The Subject of Our Lives

The Subject of Our Lives

*Thirteen San Francisco Women
Tell Their Stories*

EDITED BY

ROSEMARY PATTON

JOANN REINHARDT

SUSAN RENFREW

JEAN-LOUISE N. THACHER

1999
Fithian Press
Santa Barbara, California

Published by Fithian Press
A division of Daniel and Daniel, Publishers, Inc.
Post Office Box 1525
Santa Barbara, CA 93102

Book design: Eric Larson
Cover art: *Marmaris #3* by Nancy Genn

LIBRARY OF CONGRESS CATALOGING-IN-PUBLICATION DATA
The subject of our lives : thirteen San Francisco women tell their stories / edited by
Rosemary Patton...[et al.].
    p.   cm.
  ISBN 1-56474-270-9 (alk. paper)
  1. San Francisco (Calif.)—Biography. 2. Women—California—San Francisco—
Biography. I. Patton, Rosemary.
F869.S3S83 1999
920.72'0979461—dc21   98-4486
                                                                        CIP

To
Mary Jane Moffat
friend
and
inspiration

CONTENTS

Preface

WE STARTED WRITING AS members of the Parachutists, the metaphoric name of a San Francisco reading group with twenty-five or so members, founded in 1970 by Emily Evers and our mentor, J.J. Wilson of Sonoma State University. Thirteen of us have been writing together for over ten years and so have developed the kind of intimacy and trust that allows us to share our lives with each other. Now we want to reach a larger audience of family, friends, and even strangers, the writer in each of us seeking to be heard beyond the confines of our little band. Most of us have aimed for the "truth" as we remember our very disparate lives. One writer has turned deliberately to fiction to capture the spirit of a place. No doubt she is not alone in creating "fictions." We have been nurtured and inspired by our guide and teacher, Mary Jane Moffat. We take courage from the words of Giuseppe di Lampedusa, the Italian writer celebrated for his biographical fiction, *The Leopard:*

> When one reaches the decline of life it is imperative to try
> and gather together as many as possible of the sensations
> which have passed through our particular organism. Few can
> succeed in thus creating a masterpiece (Rousseau, Stendhal,
> Proust), but all should find it possible to preserve in some
> such way things which without this slight effort would be
> lost forever. To keep a diary, or write down one's own

memories at a certain age, should be a duty "state imposed"; material thus accumulated would have inestimable value after three or four generations; many of the psychological and historical problems that assail humanity would be resolved. There are no memoirs, even those written by insignificant people, which do not include social and graphic details of first-rate importance.

We do not consider ourselves in "the decline of life," not yet, nor would we admit to "insignificant," nor participate in his confidence that we will ameliorate the "problems that assail humanity," lovely as the claim may be. But we do share Lampedusa's enthusiasm for gathering together the "sensations" that have helped to shape our lives. As Simone de Beauvoir said, women must become the "subject" of their lives, no longer the "object" of someone else's. We have taken that step.

The Subject of Our Lives

Childhood

MARGARET GAULT

Lessons

"IT LOOKS LIKE A DOG NOW," I lied to myself silently.

The blob of damp clay didn't really look like a dog. If it re-sembled a living thing at all, it was a baby deer, a fawn. My seven-year-old stomach gurgled but no one heard. I was alone in my second-grade classroom, sitting at my desk. A piece of newspaper covered the wooden surface and on it rested the blob, awkwardly modeled. At 2:30 in the afternoon, I would ordinarily be at home from school, sitting in the breakfast room eating an apple and a cookie. But not today. Today my mother and Miss Ringer, the sec-ond-grade head teacher, were sitting in Miss Ringer's office talking quietly while I finished my statue of a dog.

Five days a week right after lunch the second grade class had art. At the University Elementary School, part of the UCLA Education Department, each grade studied a broad general subject whose theme permeated all the school work that school year. Second grade studied communities. We didn't call it that, but that's what it was. We made two-story buildings out of wooden orange crates and created a town. I don't remember what building I made, an undistinguished house, probably. The building I wished I had made was the firehouse. It had a round hole cut in the second-story floor and a wooden pole going through it from the second-story ceiling to the first-story floor for the firemen to slide down. One of the boys probably made it. You had to cut that hole out of the floor with a coping saw.

On that particular day in art, the teacher had brought a tub of clay for us to model. We had decided to make animals which would live in our orange-crate town, and I planned to make a dog. As usual, during art the students sitting around me quickly and competently created whatever they wished from the material at hand. I, on the other hand, fumbled and froze, knowing everyone else's work would be better than mine. This day was no different. Cats, dogs, canaries, guinea pigs, even horses emerged from the moist, gray, doughy clay. But I couldn't make a dog.

When the art teacher walked around the room collecting the statues and the scraps of clay, I crushed my unfinished work into a ball and placed it in the scraps tub.

"That's not where the animals go, Margaret."

"This isn't an animal. I couldn't make a dog."

The art teacher went silently on, collecting everyone else's work, then passed into Miss Ringer's office.

She came into our room, a slight silver-haired lady who always dressed in a dark suit. She wasn't much taller than the second graders, but we never thought of her as fragile. The room was filled with the bustle of children getting ready to go outdoors for recess as she came quietly up to me.

"Margaret, after school when your mother comes to pick you up I will ask her to wait in my office until you finish the dog you were making in art. We want to have a statue from you as well as from all the other children."

So after recess I returned to the empty room, where a lump of clay waited on my desk top. With the quiet, unconcerned voices of Miss Ringer and my mother in the background, I wrestled with the clay. A head emerged from one end, then what looked like haunches on the other end. It was easy to make what looked like two paws under the head as though an animal crouched. But the head refused to take on any dog-like characteristics. The ears, eyes, mouth, nose, nothing looked like a dog. I tried over and over. But it did look like an animal, although not an animal that lived in a town. Finally, I realized that I could sit at that desk forever and the statue would never become a dog. It was not that I wanted to go home before dark or that I pictured myself staying overnight in the schoolroom. It was simply that I knew I would never be able to make a dog which I could proudly display to Miss Ringer and say, "I'm finished, Miss Ringer. Here is my dog."

Picking up the piece of worked-over clay, I walked into Miss Ringer's office and said, "Here, Miss Ringer, here is the dog."

In the second grade, Miss Ringer taught me never to admit failure by insisting that I create from a blob of clay an object that I was satisfied to call a dog. Throughout my six years at University Elementary School, however, I suffered failure continuously, something I never talked about and which no one else ever noticed.

At my lab school for the UCLA Department of Education, we learned according to the precepts of John Dewey. We learned by doing. We never used conventional schoolbooks until the fifth grade, when we began to study arithmetic. But we had made and learned to use an abacus when we studied China in the fourth grade. We knew everything about measuring from creating the objects we made inspired by the general subject we studied in each school year, such objects as a wooden ship when we studied Los Angeles and its environs in the third grade. That year I made a barge and christened her "Suzy." One of my best friends, Frannie, made an ocean liner christened "Miss America" and painted red, white, and blue, red hull below the water line, white superstructure, and blue smokestacks. "Miss America" was a stunner. How I wished she were mine!

We learned history by creating a "time line" each year. The time line consisted of a horizontal line of pictures hung around the classroom just above the blackboard. These pictures were drawn by the students in our class, and sometimes by the end of the school year the time line extended all the way around all four sides of the room.

The pictures represented chronological events in the history of whatever subject we studied that year.

Only one picture was hung to illustrate each event we studied. We had art every day, and probably once a week we spent the art period drawing pictures for the time line. We could choose whatever subject we liked to draw. It was usually an illustration of an event we had studied that week, but we didn't all draw the same event. For example, in the fourth grade when we studied China, I remember the picture I drew illustrating the time we studied the wicked last empress of China. She took all the money raised from the poor peasants to build a navy, and she had a marble boat built at the Summer Palace outside Beijing for her own pleasure. The boat was so heavy it wouldn't even float and rested on the bottom of a shallow lake shore. Others in the class might have drawn the starving peasants giving their last yuan to the tax collector or some other event connected with the period.

At the end of the class, the art teacher collected the pictures, propped them up against the board in the front of the room, and the class voted on which picture was good enough to hang on the wall as the next episode of the same line. The class usually chose a short list of four or five pictures which were obviously the best, and from among those we voted formally on which one to hang. We created a time line in every grade from first through sixth. Never once in all those six years was my picture chosen for the time line. I was the only one in the class whose artwork never made it.

The anxiety I felt during those elections wells up within me just thinking about them. I never gave up hope. Two or three times a semester my picture would be part of the short list of drawings propped up in the blackboard tray for the class to vote on. I tried every good luck charm I knew to make my picture the chosen one. I sat with my hands in my lap, all fingers on both hands crossed, and my ankles crossed under the table. I held my breath for the entire length of the voting, all the while trying to look like I was distracted by the leaves outside the window flickering in the wind. I prayed fervently, "Dear Lord, please make them choose my picture. If You make it happen just this once, I will never ask for anything again. Amen."

But that particular prayer was never answered. Perhaps Miss Ringer's lesson about not admitting failure was what kept me quiet about my failure to make the time line. Actually, it was not failure. One person "won" each time in that his or her picture was judged the best, and all the rest of us "lost" in that we all came in second. I don't believe anyone else kept track like I did. Everyone else had at least one picture up there in the six years, even Janet Kinninger, a poor little dumpling who was probably slightly Mongoloid and who did not return after vacation to the fifth grade. Janet had died during the summer. Of course, Patricia Wynn had many, many pictures hung each year. That was okay. Her mother was an artist and Patricia drew beautifully flowing color, sharp perspective and angles into the pictures which gave her room enough to illustrate real drama in a very small space.

Six years went by and I never called attention to my intense yearning to join the artists of the time line. I never told my mother, my friends, my teachers, anyone. In fact, almost sixty years went by and then I told my classmates, many whom are as close friends now as they were then, keeping up connections being one of the great advantages of attending this particular school. To my surprise, shock and disappointment, their reactions sounded like this, "You never had a picture on the time line! What a tragedy! How have you lived all these years?" "I never won the fifty-yard dash in our track meets and I managed to survive anyway." "You may not have been a good artist, but your plays were chosen to be performed, your lyrics used in the songs we wrote. Get real, Margaret. You won't get any sympathy from us about the time lines." I thought they would empathize with my deep feelings and fervent desires to succeed as an artist, but they did not.

Oh, well.

JOANN REINHARDT

Soaps and Sympathy

IN THE 1930s AND '40s parents took children's illness very seriously. There was no penicillin, no broad-spectrum antibiotics, no sulfa. When you got sick you went to bed. If you had a fever, you didn't get up until your fever had been gone for twenty-four hours.

In my family, we three children usually had all the childhood diseases at more or less the same time. When my brother started school he brought home chicken pox, and my older sister and I both caught it. We put calamine lotion on our dolls as well as ourselves, and Mother read aloud to us to pass the time.

We went through a lot of childhood diseases together. We sat around in our pajamas and nightgowns, not feeling very sick, compared spots, bumps or swollen glands, and ate milk toast and drank Ovaltine.

(My brother was saving the thin metal seals from under the lid of each can of Ovaltine to send in for a mystery decoder pin from Little Orphan Annie, who came to us on the radio in the late afternoon, just after "Jack Armstrong, the All-American Boy.")

If the disease was serious enough, my parents put a "Quarantine" sign on our door so the milkman or laundry man wouldn't come in for a chat.

We almost never went to a doctor's office. When we saw a doctor, it was because he came to our house. It was a sort of ritual of confirmation—"Yes, this family seems to have measles." Much more frightening were bad ears, tonsillitis and very bad stomach aches in the lower right side of the abdomen, which might mean appendicitis.

With a temperature, we had to go to bed at once. I had visions of good armies fighting the bad infections, but only if you were horizontal. Mother was always solicitous, with wash rags wrung out in cold water for our hot foreheads and sometimes sheets fresh from the laundry. In the late afternoon, Mother read to us. *Alice in Wonderland* was a great favorite of hers—but not, in fact, of ours. Sometimes she read *When We Were Very Young* or *A Child's Garden of Verses*. We also loved the poems of James Whitcomb Riley. He was from Indiana too, and we were loyal to fellow Hoosiers. I thought all Hoosiers were related.

Best of all, we loved to have her tell us stories of her childhood in the South. She had two stories we wanted to hear over and over. One was about the night when her father's buggy factory caught on fire. The other concerned the day she was driving a horse and buggy and the horse ran away while she was holding the reins. The story always ended the same way: "The harder I tugged at the reins, the faster the horse went. I didn't know he had been trained as a race horse!" It seemed to us that nothing that exciting happened to children anymore.

When I was six years old, we moved to Southern California to find a milder climate for my father, who had heart disease. We children continued with our usual childhood diseases, and by the time I was nine I had had them all and more—chicken pox, mumps, measles, scarlet fever, whooping cough. Nothing was left to catch except routine colds and stomach aches and flu, but these allowed me time at home, where I had Mother to myself and could catch up on the soap operas.

Our family's general rule was that if you were sick enough to be home from school, you were sick enough to be in bed. Actually, I loved being sick enough to stay home. Early in the morning, usually before my father's gentle wake-up call (he always woke us individually), I knew I would be staying home that day. No talk about which dress, what color hair ribbon, no lunch box filled with chopped olive sandwiches and celery sticks, no running to catch the school bus. Instead, I snuggled down in bed, waiting for Mother to "get the others off," meaning my father and my brother and sister. I could feel the rushing and hear the talking. In my room it was peaceful and almost lonely, and I hoped I wasn't missing anything in the breakfast room downstairs. Finally and abruptly, with the last door slam, everything was quiet. I was in a mysterious world: my own house when I wasn't there.

Soon Mother would appear with a breakfast tray with orange juice and hot chocolate and perhaps French toast. Balancing the tray and not spilling wasn't easy. I always wanted a bed tray with legs, a wicker one like my Aunt Elizabeth had, but we never got one. I think Mother felt there was no point in making room service too attractive. Along with the tray came "sit-up" pillows and the little radio from the kitchen and the funny papers, as we used to call them. I liked "Li'l Abner" and "Dick Tracy" and "Grin and Bear It."

Around nine o'clock, a piano playing "Clair de Lune" on the radio announced "The Story of Mary Marlin," and the beginning of a heavy day of soap operas to help me forget my sore throat or my aches and fever. After fifteen minutes of Mary Marlin came "The Romance of Helen Trent," asking each day: "Can a woman find romance in life at thirty-five and *even beyond*?" Actually, Helen seemed to have lots of boyfriends, but I wasn't quite sure what romance was, except probably dancing in nightclubs.

Next came Oxydol's own "Ma Perkins" and "Pepper Young's Family," both featuring middle-aged women who gave their friends and family lots of advice, which the friends and family seemed grateful to get. Around 11:00, "Our Gal Sunday," with "Red River Valley" on the harmonica as its theme song, asked: "Can this girl from a little mining town in the West find happiness as the wife of England's richest, most handsome lord, Lord Henry Brinthrop?"

Year after year, the answer seemed in doubt. Mother did not join me in following these endless stories. The only daytime program she liked was "Vic and Sade," which was funny and plotless and did not have a daily crisis.

At noon there was a trilogy I liked very much—"Pretty Kitty Kelly" (theme song, "Oh, the Days of the Kerry Dances!" played on the organ), "Myrt and Marge," and "Hilltop House," the episodic story of an orphanage.

By then Mother would have brought a lunch tray: an open-faced sandwich with the crusts cut off and perhaps some soup—but no milk if you had a cold. If you had an upset stomach, you drank Coca-Cola or ginger ale and ate only soda crackers until your stomach had settled down.

Usually, the afternoon in bed was more trying than the morning. The bed pillows got hot and there were crumbs in the sheets. Sometimes Mother had to go out on errands, and I felt deserted and cranky. The afternoon soap operas were a comfort—"Life Can Be Beautiful," with ChiChi Baby and Papa David, and "Just Plain Bill, Barber of Hartville." A guitar played the theme song, "Nita, Juanita." And there was "Mr. Keene, Tracer of Lost Persons," whose theme was "Someday, I'll Find You" and "Road of Life" (introduced by Tchaikovsky's sixth symphony, with a voice saying, "Doctor Brent, call surgery," in the background). I had pretty much lost my power of concentration by the time "Light of the World, the Story of the Bible" and "Stella Dallas" came on. (Stella's daughter, Lolly-Baby, had married above her mother's station in life.)

Soon my sister would come home with news from school and from the rest of that distant outside world that I so quickly felt removed from. If I seemed to be "on the mend," Mother would suggest I "try my legs" and sit in the den for a while. I felt special and fragile, wandering around the house in my nightgown and slippers, visiting the rooms like a stranger. Before long I usually was back in bed, having a light supper, "because you shouldn't eat too much just before going to sleep."

After the rest of the family had eaten dinner, they settled into their usual pattern of homework and telephone calls—the phone's twenty-five-foot cord snaked through halls and into bedrooms for privacy—and favorite radio programs: Jimmy Fiddler's gossip about Hollywood (my sister's favorite), Fred Waring and his glee club, and sometimes Henry Aldrich. My mother would come and remake my bed and bring me hot chocolate with marshmallows, and she would feel my brow for signs of fever. My father would play a game with me or read me an Uncle Remus story. (Even when I was older, I loved his tales of Uncle Remus.)

Then Daddy would turn out the light. Lying there I could hear the voices downstairs and the country music of Stuart Hamblin and His Boys coming faintly from my brother's room. The bed felt cool and tidy now, and somehow smaller without the "sit-up" pillows. I went to sleep feeling a little like a pampered princess but knowing all the while that it would be someone else's turn next time.

ROSEMARY PATTON

Out of the Garden

DEIRDRE AND I ARE SITTING on the lawn at Greycraig with our new friends Jeannie and Annie, sisters like ourselves, seven and eight years old. They are subdued and watchful, waiting for cues as they follow our lead in every step of the afternoon. A very British tea is laid out on a wool rug in front of us. It is late August 1942, Scotland. Greycraig was the third in the series of country houses our American mother had collected since 1933, when, after five years of marriage to a wandering British naval officer, she moved into the first such house, in rural Oxfordshire. Expecting her second child, me, she had declared it time to settle down. "No more traveling with children," as she still puts it, three more children and eleven houses later.

Greycraig was the first house they had owned, this time to house three daughters and now a new baby boy. We moved in the week before John arrived on June 30, leaving with regret the remote moorland shooting "cottage" of the previous year after our mother's obstetrician pointed out the obvious—she would need electricity and easier access to medical care with a new baby, not to mention schools for Deirdre and me, absent from school for a year. As it was, a baby was an experiment, a necessary wartime experiment, for my mother, used as she was to nannies in the past.

She had decided on Greycraig on impulse, trusting herself, as has always been her wont. Our father raised no objections. The location was relatively safe from bombs, the price, reflecting wartime real estate, absurdly low. When my mother went to her banker to discuss a loan, he smiled and said she could simply carry the sum as an overdraft. Banking and real estate have changed a little since then. My father was en route to a two-year assignment in North Africa, lucky to catch a glimpse of his tiny son before departure. The house of gray Scottish stone stood foursquare, strong, imposing, yet inviting. A slight curve to the broad front added grace. But randomly sealed-over windows, large, smooth and gray, gave a strange imbalance to the façade. A window tax in years past had led to many a covered-over window in Scotland. Our mother loved the spacious, airy, high-ceilinged rooms so beautifully proportioned—a little more lovable in the spring and summer, when she found the house, than on freezing winter evenings to come. We were to spend many hours huddled in the kitchen around the big coal-fired range, the fabled Aga Cooker richly clad in cream-colored porcelain, or in front of fireplaces. We usually dressed under the covers. But that was later. She had also been seduced by the elegantly decorated Robert Adam ceilings, convinced they were from the hand of the celebrated eighteenth-century Scottish architect himself. We were only a short distance north of Edinburgh, in Fife, and the Adam brothers had grown up nearby. She may have been right.

Situated on a gentle slope, the house faced south and was surrounded by spacious gardens, some dense woods, and several acres of fields beyond. These last were leased to the local farmer, but the gardens and the beech wood dropping steeply to the Black Devon, our own little reach of river, provided a magical playground for Deirdre and me and for Elgiva, four years older, when she wasn't away in boarding school. We grew increasingly annoyed that no one could put the deserted clay tennis court in playing order. Grass grew in the crevices, the net was disintegrating, the giant iron roller grew rustier with each year. And the absence of horses in the stables remained a quiet disappointment. But we never really believed that these omissions could be righted, any more than we believed that the war would one day be over, that our father would spend time at home again, or that we would one day grow up. Young as we were, we sensed that our mother, even with the help of Mr. Hunchinson, the elderly gardener, could not bring us horses and tennis parties in this still-remote corner at this time in history. And we knew for sure that young Mr. Graham, the surly fellow who appeared occasionally to repair our electric generator when the huge leather belt flew off the wheels, would be more likely to sabotage than secure such luxuries. Why he had escaped military service remained a mystery. Perhaps he was too ornery.

Occasionally, again in the future, the fruit in the walled orchard and, at Christmas, the holly growing near the road offered irresistible temptations to youths, both boys and girls, from the village a mile away. Class-consciousness was soon to enter our protected lives.

But I have stranded four little girls sitting in the August sun on a rug on a lawn. We have played outside for some time, shared our bicycles—although I don't think they knew how to ride them—and eaten the bread and butter, biscuits, and cake. We have drunk, I am sure, lemon squash rather than the usual milk. But we are not satisfied. Although I remember only silence from Jeannie and Annie, Deirdre and I are delighted to have friends come to our house, children beyond sisters to play with, and we want to show them our toys, to take them into our large playroom and introduce them to our dolls, our books, our games. This desire creates a problem.

As the elder and the more outspoken of the two, I, though blissfully unaware at that age, could annoy my elders if their desires conflicted with mine. Especially cherished by our nanny for five years and always treated even-handedly by our mother, I was not predisposed for censure by more critical caretakers. On this occasion we are not in the hands of our mother.

She is upstairs in the drawing room or resting in her bedroom or administering to John, adjusting to her new role as mother of an infant still too young to be exposed to other children, especially these two little visitors, daughters of a coal miner. The obligatory baby nurse has just left after her six weeks. Gwen deRincey, an old friend, childless and available, has come up from England to supervise Deirdre and me and do the cooking for a few weeks until our mother gets the hang of things. Domestic help was hard to come by during the war. I was unaware until years later that Gwen did not take well to me and was urged, on some pretext, to leave early so that I would not be warped by her displeasure. I do remember my fury when she pulled my curly hair and splashed water in my ears while washing my hair. But I also adored her beautiful white cat, not a favorite of our mother, was intrigued by the photo of her tall husband with his hand resting on the head of a giant German shepherd, and recall our amusement at some of her jokes and pronouncements. She would rather have her head cut off than eat chocolate before breakfast. We thought that delightfully funny. We were also profoundly interested in why her hair was already white and why she had no children. I was probably the one who posed these questions. No wonder she found me less than adorable.

My pleas to be allowed inside are met with a firm "No." "Why?" I respond. Not, in that era, the sign of admirable curiosity. At first she tries the easy route. John is too tiny and can't be exposed to other children's germs. I won't settle for this. Another child had been there the week before, inside the sacred house. Gwen is inexperienced with childish wiles. She is better suited to coping with Deirdre, who is smart enough to keep her own counsel and let me be the argumentative one. She has always been better at assessing which battles are worth fighting, which better left alone. Gwen is growing frustrated. Jeannie and Annie are staring up from the lawn, their faces perfect little blanks.

Gwen draws me aside. In the kind of loud whisper that can be heard yards away, she cautions me.

"You will only make them unhappy if you take them inside and show them all your toys. They are not as fortunate as you. You need to understand this. Don't talk about it anymore. Soon it will be time for them to go home." I don't understand and yet I do. I am furious. My precious little will has been thwarted. I am embarrassed. I am confused. I begin to sense things that will grow clearer as I grow older. Injustice, even then, is palpable.

My mother was insulated from this exchange at the time, although I am sure I would have complained to her about it later, without realizing that the incident had grown out of one of her latest enthusiasms, the much-heralded Scottish educational system. Elgiva, who had just turned thirteen, was on her third carefully selected school, all in England, where we had lived until the year before. Waiting for Deirdre, a year younger, I had stayed home the first year I was supposed to go to school, and we had "studied," very ineffectively, with a rather disagreeable governess. At six and a half, still living in the Oxfordshire house, I went with both sisters and two older cousins to a nearby convent school. I had company in playing the role of outsider, but had my first taste of being different as a Protestant in a Catholic school. A year later we found ourselves on the Scottish moors, where Deirdre and I had no school except for the game of school we so often played, usually in the old quarry, where the steady drip down the rock served as our clock.

When we moved to Greycraig, we were eager to start school in Saline, the state-run elementary school a mile's walk from Greycraig. You had to live more than a mile from the nearest village or bus line before being eligible for the precious petrol ration, so that mile was to become agonizingly familiar over the four years we traveled it.

While Greycraig was replete with comfortable grandeur and bucolic setting, Saline reflected the socioeconomic fabric of the community, something our parents seemed not to have noticed when they purchased the house. Set on the edge of a series of active coal mines, the village was a scrappy place, populated by miners, a few others whose businesses supported that enterprise and a modest handful of the more fortunate—the owner of the local mines, a couple of landowners, and a few rungs down, the doctor, the rector of the Presbyterian church, and the school headmaster. Along the main road out of town, dismal slag heaps rose behind dilapidated housing blocks. Saline did not qualify for books on the picturesque villages of Britain. At that time, our district sent the only communist to Parliament, the fiery Willy Gallagher.

The houses were, for the most part, dispiriting—small, hot, crowded, mean. A huge double bed and an open coal stove prevailed in most living rooms into which the front door usually opened, often down a few steps from the street. Most families remained poor, in part because salaries were low, and because miners were notoriously partial to drinking and gambling on the dog races every weekend, or so we were indoctrinated. Their children attended the local school until they were fourteen and then became adults overnight. The boys "went down in the pit," the girls worked in the shops, such as they were, curled their hair, and soon married. We were instructed not to enter these houses.

Deirdre and I walked into this setting in July. The usually short British summer vacation was even shorter here because two weeks were reserved for October, when school children helped with the potato picking during the war—the "tatty-picking holiday." We were fascinated and appalled by what we found at school. The bathrooms were to be avoided at all costs, more like barnyards than anything we had experienced. The two- (or was it three-?) story building was functional but stark and depressing. The playground was cramped and paved, with an iron fence dividing girls from boys—a far cry from the rolling lawns, flowers, and tennis courts of the convent. The children appeared at first either rough and tough or pathetically puny. Some arrived at school barefoot. No one commented. Strangely, we did not reveal details to our mother at first.

But we were pleased when our classmates greeted us with friendship in spite of our English accents and what must have been startling contrasts to the often glaring poverty of many. Perhaps it helped that we were both behind in the school curriculum. I remember a more able peer assigned to bring me up to scratch in arithmetic. Her name is gone, but her short blond hair and sweet face can creep up beside me still when I do subtraction or division. I

was not, apparently, the most able student, because I recently discovered that I follow a peculiar process for subtraction known to no
one else, not even Deirdre. Reading was no problem, but I can still
break out in a cold sweat when I think about the written exercises
and essays that were first produced in chalk on slates. I had little ap-
titude for and no remembered instruction in spelling. And I was un-
familiar with chalk. The combination proved disastrous. Each day
that we were to transcribe our work from slate to exercise book with
scratchy pens dipped in desk inkwells, I would find most of my work
either indecipherable or partially smudged and erased. Teachers bur-
dened with huge classes of often unruly children were short on patience. Miss McCormick was not delighted with my performance.
Learning was proving to be less than agreeable.

We had little if any homework, and once outside the classroom I
enjoyed this odd new life. A classmate, Jenny Kenny, took me with
her during lunch to visit her aunt, always in bed and reeking of what
I was later to realize was a steady addiction to the bottle. I delighted
in the confidences of this carefree little spirit with lush long hair
who so quickly befriended me. I knew my mother would never know
that I entered the forbidden houses. I quickly fell in love with
Jenny's older brother Patrick, a slim, sinewy blond of nine for whom
I had to declare my affection. A popular recess game, organized by
the older girls, had a group form a circle and sing a song as the
circle moved around the chosen one, who had to name the boy of
her dreams. As new material, I was often singled out and was too naive to disguise my feelings and was undoubtedly pleased by the attention.

> The wind, the wind, the wind blows high, the rain is falling
> from the sky. Patrick Kenny says he loves her, all the boys
> are fighting for her, don't care what the boys say....

And on it went, voices thick with Scottish brogues. Through the
iron fence, groups of brawling boys would whoop and holler in response to our songs. Patrick never declared his love for me, alas, but

he never complained about being singled out, either. Betty Allen, daughter of a miner, who at fourteen had finished school and had come to work as a daily babysitter for my brother John, assured me that the Kenny family were of Irish origin, known thieves, and beneath contempt. But nothing ever changed my devotion, especially when a year later Betty was dismissed for increasing incompetence. Deirdre and I missed the steady stream of gossip she brought with her each day.

The toughest girl, Nanny by name and a couple of years older than I, took Deirdre and me under her protection, and the foul-mouthed boys treated us with respect. We had summoned enough courage to invite sisters Jeannie and Annie to play. At the appointed hour, they went home, as Gwen said they would, no doubt alone on foot. Gwen planted the first seed of disquiet in our minds. We had been accepted into an alien world, but it was going to be more difficult to accept members of this new world into ours. I postponed inviting the wilder Jenny.

Gwen left. My mother gradually got wind of the real world of the Saline school. So much for Scottish public education. What remains in memory as a mini-lifetime lasted only three months. The important lessons I learned did not come from our textbooks or from the terrifying chalk and slate.

Our mother discovered Dollar Academy, a remarkable private school seven or eight miles away, and had us transferred there just before the tatty-picking holiday. We wore uniforms. We never sang "The wind, the wind, the wind blows high." We waited in Saline every morning for the bus that passed through on its way between Dunfirmline and Dollar. And every day during the Saline school holiday late that October, either morning or late afternoon, as we walked the quiet country mile to or from our house, we would meet the Saline school children going to or from the potato fields. Overnight we had become the enemy, the rich girls who lived in the big house and went to Dollar Academy. No longer did we live in the safety of their approval. They relished the threatening insults they hurled our way, their Scottish voices mocking, snarling, and they laughed as they pointed at us and then at the animal dung along the rural road. We cowered and turned our heads, Deirdre moving up closer to me from her customary place a few feet behind. We were finding out what it meant to live in more than one world, to have one's personal definition begin to grow fuzzy around the edges. We knew it was complicated and could never confide our fears to our mother.

JOANN REINHARDT

Working for Willkie

OUR FAMILY WAS REPUBLICAN. I can't remember hearing any discussion about the matter. It was just that we rooted for the Republicans as we rooted for Indiana University to win basketball and football games. We were Republicans the way we were Presbyterians and Midwesterners.

I didn't know it was possible to change sides until my sister announced during the 1936 presidential election, when she was eleven, that she was not for Alf Landon, the Republican candidate. We were traveling from our new home in California across the country that summer, visiting friends and family in Indianapolis and picking up a new Ford from the factory in Michigan before starting the long trip back to the West.

All along the way we crisscrossed the route of the presidential trains on their whistle-stop tours. At one of the stops, we saw Governor Landon on the deck of an observation car. After his speech he tossed out campaign buttons shaped like little sunflowers. Landon was from Kansas, the sunflower state, so I knew we were "for" him and, of course, we were also "against" Roosevelt. Midwestern Republicans hated Roosevelt. They called him "that man" so they would not have to speak his name.

My older brother, who had just turned thirteen, and I scooped up all the sunflower buttons we could grab. We kept them in the car all the way back to California because they had been touched by a man who might become president. My sister wouldn't pick up any of the buttons. She said she wished she had stayed in the car. Even at age eight I suspected that Alf Landon had little chance to win. I think that was one reason my sister said she was for Roosevelt. She liked to be on the winning side, and she also liked to make up her own mind.

It was a different story four years later when my father's old friend and fraternity brother, Wendell Willkie, began to be talked about as a Republican candidate for President. My father admired Willkie, who had been a successful businessman. He thought Willkie was strong, principled, and had a world view that some Republicans lacked.

Our whole family lived and breathed Willkie's campaign for nomination that July. My father drew up a tally of all the states, and he and my sister took turns recording the numbers as we listened to the radio broadcast of the convention while the delegates were casting their votes.

"The great state of Alabama casts its votes.... The Sunshine State.... The Patriot State.... Illinois, the state of Abraham Lincoln.... The Golden State...." The field was open, and the speeches were long. Roosevelt was going for an unprecedented third term. War in Europe was a possibility, and feelings ran high among the Republicans.

As the convention moved along, it became clear even to us children that Willkie's chief rivals were Robert Taft, Jr., and Thomas Dewey. At our command post in the den, there was always someone listening to the convention on the radio. Sometimes all five of us were there. My sister and I sat in shorts and halters, drinking iced tea and wild with excitement as slowly the numbers began to climb for Willkie. The delegates chanted, "We want Willkie!" Even our adolescent, sixteen-year-old brother, who at that moment hated

Ruthie and me, rejoined the family from his room for the final bal-
loting, the victory, and the demonstration.

The rest of my summer was devoted to Wendell Willkie. My father was appointed Southern California chairman of the Willkie
campaign and took a leave from his office for the three months before the election. Because I liked collecting things, I immediately
started a Willkie button collection. (I still had my Landon buttons.)
Daddy often took me with him that summer when he met with
people in the campaign, and I always picked up a few new buttons. I
had all the ordinary buttons that said "Win with Willkie" or
"Marion County Indiana for Willkie," and also the harder-to-come-
by, meaner ones that said "I Don't Want Eleanor, Either" or "I
Want to Be a Captain, Too," referring to FDR's son, James, who had
received an instant commission in the Army. I liked the mean ones
best because I was so partisan.

Late in the summer Wendell and Edith Willkie came to California. My whole family went to the Biltmore Hotel in Los Angeles to
meet them. That evening there was to be a rally at the Hollywood
Bowl. We sat in one of the boxes and ate a cold fried chicken picnic
that mother had made. After dinner Daddy was to go onto the stage
to sit with the dignitaries and celebrities.

During supper he said he really didn't care about sitting on the
stage. He thought it would be fun for one of us children to take his
place. We drew straws, and for the first time, ever, I drew the long
one.

I couldn't believe that I had won. I thought I could never win
against my brother and sister. I was sure my sister would say that she
didn't care and that she hadn't wanted to sit there, anyway. Instead,
Bud and Ruthie only made the half-hearted suggestion that maybe I
would be scared, being there all by myself.

Daddy took me by the hand down through the wings of the
stage and showed me where my seat was. I felt very alone. There I
was on the platform of the Hollywood Bowl, the only child on a
stage filled with adults, a small, brown-haired, freckle-faced, twelve-
year-old girl with a big smile and a chest full of Willkie buttons. I

felt people staring at me. Was I a movie star whose familiar face had slipped their minds? Certainly not Shirley Temple. Hair too light for Jane Withers. Not Margaret O'Brien, either, although the freckles were right. And too young for Deanna Durbin.

I sat there quietly, remembering to keep my knees together, trying to see past the floodlights into the gloom where I knew my family was sitting. Suddenly, I didn't care that I couldn't find them. I was on the stage with lots of famous people, enjoying the warm summer night and the loudspeaker and the applause. I had always looked forward to being an adult, and this was perhaps the first really grown-up thing that had happened to me.

In November Wendell Willkie lost the election. I was very sad for him and for my father who had worked so hard. It was over so quickly, and the end was so final, that all I had left of my summer campaign was my Willkie button collection and my optimism. Just wait until 1944!

BETTY WHITRIDGE

Only Child Leaves Arkansas, Enters Arlington

BELOVED GRANDPARENTS, "Mam-Mam" and "Omer" Bird had me and my mother, their beautiful young daughter-in-law Isabelle, living with them in their big old rambly white house. Isabelle gallantly supported her only child—Dutch-bobbed, brown-eyed, four-year-old me by teaching first grade in the public school of our sleepy small town: Waldron, County Seat of Scott County, Arkansas. Mam-Mam and Omer cherished and spoiled their adored only grandchild—me.

A few blocks up the street (dirt road, actually) lived Mother's father, the important Judge Samuel Knox Duncan with his silly second wife, Miss Maggie, whom I called Miss Magazine. The Duncans vied with the Birds, outdoing each other in coddling, presents, attentions lavished on their only Arkansas grandchild—me.

I was the *only* child amongst all the extended family. All my childless uncles, aunts, childless Bird and Duncan cousins, childless great aunts and uncles, all of whom lived in the town, competed for my time and favor. Daddy was infrequently around. As such an indulged, admired, only child, I must have been dreadfully spoiled and difficult—tho' I only remember being thought charming!!

I was too young to be in school (four and a half, probably) but considered "so smart" that I was stuck in anyway. Or maybe it wasn't my suspected brilliance that got me matriculated—just a simple solution to the teacher-mother's childcare situation. I was a notorious problem in Mother's class, scorning the routine, vetoing the games. I refused to sing the songs though I knew them all by heart, warbling them constantly for all the admiring kinfolk at home. I adamantly disdained to read a word even though the family considered me a phenomenon for the way I read outside of school. I made the teacher-mother's school days a nightmare, always doing the wrong thing, embarrassing her in front of the other teachers and the legitimate pupils. Anyway, it didn't work out.

Quietly, mysteriously, I found myself and my mother on a train for days and days and days. There had been no kinfolk, friends or bon voyage sayers; it was all rather hush-hush. The surprising, and to me murky and interminable, trip was actually only five days, I think. It seemed an eternity to a bewildered, cooped-up child. The only child on the train, of course. My oft-quoted mot from this journey was a long sigh: "Ohhhhh, I didn't know there was so *much* earth."

The destination, or the reason, for this furtive fleeing was never explained to me. I think I was sort of kidnapped, or at least bundled away from the Birds. Finally this prison of a train disgorged us in Seattle.

Mother's brother, my taciturn, droll, witty Uncle Edgar Duncan, a recent John's Hopkins graduate, was practicing medicine in Seattle. He met us at the train and took us to his apartment. There, I promptly, obligingly, came down with a severe case of malaria. Pretty awful for Isabelle who'd fled here for shelter and hadn't a penny except what Grandaddy Duncan had given her for what he evidently judged to be a necessary, urgent exodus from Arkansas. Malaria is, or was then, common in Arkansas, but unheard of in Seattle. Uncle Edgar was pleased to be able to provide a clinical treat for all his medical cronies. What a treat! He'd bring them around to observe this disease unknown to them. Notebooks in hand, they'd

stand by my sweaty bed watching me alternately burn up, throw off
the sheets, shake, shiver, freeze, pile on the blankets. They had the
audacity to take notes and discuss the symptoms whilst amazedly
checking my soaring temperature. I recall, through the haze of ague,
feeling rather annoyed at being the star of this side show.

The bitter, acrid taste of quinine, the only known malaria remedy in those dark pre-miracle drug days, still lingers in my mouth
and memory. There was no Mam-Mam's special cooking, no cud-
dling with my dear dog Trumpet, no presents from Sugar and Mac,
no wonderful stories from the spellbinding folktale spinner, Aunt
Ree, no hugs or pennies from Omer. Just bone-rattling chills, followed by 106-degree temperature, peering medicos, worried mother
in strange, lonely surroundings. This was not a happy time for a dis-
possessed small princess.

After our great train migration west, the Great Depression was
in full swing. Poor Isabelle, the excellent teacher, desperately
searched for a school teaching position. One, at last, presented itself
in Arlington, Washington, a small, pretty town some 90 miles north
of Seattle. When I had sufficiently recovered from the last malarial
bout, we moved to this other small sleepy town.

Small and sleepy, but otherwise unlike Waldron, Arlington sits
west of, but very near, the craggy, alpine, snowy Cascade range.
Beautiful but very *un*-Arkansas-ish.

What a change for Isabelle and Betty! In the 1920s, Arlington
was still redolent of its lusty, lumberjack origin. Unlike long settled
Waldron, everyone in Arlington was recently from somewhere else.
"No one knew their grandparents," Mother said. All of the country-
side and the town had been settled by hearty, strong Scandanavians:
Norwegians, Swedes, Danes. Many of the children in the schools
did not hear English at home. As in Waldron, children were brought
in from farms and woods to the Arlington Unified School District.
The big era of logging was over, the Depression was there, hard
times gripped the town.

We were the "rich ones" because mother had a job. True, she
was paid only in "warrants," which she had to sell to get money. Not

much money, but we did have some. Often it was hard to get the banks or anyone else to buy the warrants; then there was no money.

Once again, I was in first grade and once again my mother was my teacher. Older and wiser, this time I was ready to learn. I also renounced trying to run my mother's classroom. But there were certain adjustments to be made in this strange new land. Other children laughed at me because I said "Howdy" instead of hello. I was furious once when I guessed the correct answer to a riddle. The answer was "frying pan." I'd said skillet. My answer was rejected. I thought they were both unfair and stupid.

First of all—and amazingly—Mother and I lived in the "Royal Hotel" on Main Street of "downtown" Arlington. It was far from royal—indeed, it was a sort of flop house for old retired loggers. The townspeople considered it incredible that this pretty, young, husbandless teacher and her vulnerable little daughter would move into such a place. I think that we were perfectly safe. All the other Royal family (all elderly men) treated us with obvious respect, even adulation. Of course, I was the *only* Royal child but then, the "onlyness" role was not new to me.

Charlie Ellis, one of the oldest of the old men, became my best friend and I his. Charlie had white hair, white beard, white mustache, soft voice, roly-poly build. I thought he looked like Santa Claus. He *was* like Santa Claus. He gave me many little presents, as well as frequent treats from Mrs. Shoemaker's candy store across the street. Once he gave me a golden-haired doll as large as I was. Another of the men had a crystal radio set that he rigged up and I got to listen to the magical sounds. Alas, I fear that I was daily called upon to sing the "Ching-a Ling Chinaman" song for the old men. (Surely my fame can't have preceded me—*someone* must have volunteered me. Was it Isabelle or was it the singer herself?) This silly ditty was received with tremendous acclamation and, I blush to record, often a hail of pennies. The Royal press agents spread the news and I can remember being asked to sing it for Mr. Cady at the drug store, Dr. Leach, the town physician, and Mr. Sessoms, the banker.

Meals at the Royal were boarding house style served up by Mr.

and Mrs. Suttles, the resident owners-chefs-janitors-maids of this remarkable establishment. Three squares a day at a long lumberjack-style table to the old men and Isabelle and Betty. How I wish I had a picture of this.

In summer, we returned to Seattle to Uncle Edgar's apartment in the "La Amorita," a Spanish-style, red-roofed, towered, balconied building, quiet and pleasant with lawns and flowers, near beautiful Volunteer Park, and overlooking sylvan Lake Union. Now it can still be seen, a somewhat seedy dowager, sitting right on the I-5 Freeway, above a Lake Union crammed with planes, boatyards, and boats, with many offices, restaurants, warehouses along the shore. City things the small-town girl got to do there: theater, Woodland Park Zoo, ferry boat rides, and Frederick & Nelson, the world's most glorious department store, where ladies wore hats and gloves for tea in the dining room. Uncle Edgar took us for drives in his enormous black Lincoln—*very slow drives*. He must have been the world's slowest driver—one would think a serious occupational hazard for an obstetrician.

Mother's teaching contract was, of course, renewed. She was a famously good teacher, and besides, lots of teachers didn't seek work in bankrupt school districts that could only issue warrants instead of paychecks. Also, of course, the proper Arlingtonians wouldn't hear of her residing in the Royal Hotel any longer. We were taken in as boarders by a simple, poor family, the Bluemkes—Otto, Hattie, their children Chester and Dorothy—who lived next door to Mother's school. Once when Mother was sick in a Seattle hospital, good-hearted Hattie kept me. To cheer me up and ready me for my visit to Mother, Hattie made me an incredible cretonne dress. It had gigantic flowers, rows, tiers, froths of ruffles each trimmed with flashily multicolored bias binding, topped off magnificently by an enormous Bertha collar. I was flushed with joy and pride over this garment so different from my usual conservative middys or smocked dresses. Mother burst out laughing as I was led into her hospital room and gasped: "Oh Betty, you are too big and bulky for ruffles." Hattie and I were both crushed.

Later, we were boarders with a nice family, the prosperous Hawleys, who took us in as their civic duty. They became Mother's lifelong friends. Mother and Mrs. Hawley belonged with pride to P.E.O. We lived in our own rooms at the Hawleys, ate with them (that's what boarders *do*), went on picnics with their family and friends. On weekends and for all of every summer we went back to Seattle. There Mother cooked and cleaned Uncle Edgar's apartment. When I was a bit older, Mother scraped together money for me, the child prodigy, to have singing and violin lessons at the prestigious Cornish School. Every Sunday night in the school year, she would rush us back to Arlington and her teaching.

Our permanent home in Arlington became the Moran Apartments, also on Main Street, as was the Royal Hotel. There were lots of other children in the town, but I was the *only* child living on Main Street; all the other children had houses and families. The Moran Apartments were upstairs above a store and the Arlington Post Office. The old-maid postmistress had an unforgettable name, Bessie Snoddy, and often gave me cookies when I fetched our mail. In the Moran Apartments, no more kindly old loggers. Each and every apartment was occupied by an Arlington School teacher. All of them were spinsters except my mother. Therefore I was again, or still, guess what?—the *only* child. It was an enviable position. I had tea with Georgia Harris, the high school P.E. coach, Swedish cookies with attractive Liv Meyers, the Latin teacher. I laughed with my mother over Beulah Griep (another unforgettable name), the maiden lady high school typing teacher who turned on her light to warm up her room. Alice Satre, the English teacher, read me stories. Marjorie Duryee, the cultivated, glamorous Mills graduate, became my idol and mentor. Tina Moran boasted a marvelous locked storeroom where no one but me ever went. I could go, open Mother's big black steamer trunk and exhume all the nostalgic Arkansas things— memories of my vanished princessdom. I played with dresses, toys, photo albums, pictures, letters, lace, slippers, fur. I missed all the Arkansas kinfolk and old friends, but oddly enough the trunk sessions never made me sad, only happy.

Mother or Uncle Edgar never talked about my daddy and I never heard from him. I think that when Mother first spirited me away from Arkansas, none of the Birds knew where we were. Later, I had letters, cards, small gifts from them. Later still, we went back many times to visit them all. Some of them even braved the wild, wild West and came to see us.

The Moran Apartments had one and only one telephone, in the hall on the wall. As I grew older and could reach the phone, almost all the calls were for me. The spinster teacher ladies all teased me about my long conversations, the boys who called, the excuses I used. They could hear it all.

In the scruffy, fenced-in, untended back yard of the Moran Apartments, I planted and tended a little garden which I really enjoyed. (Perhaps this was the beginning of my addiction to gardening later in life.) Abutting the "garden" was the Greyhound Bus Depot—an important fixture of small town America in the twenties and thirties. Everybody, everything came and went from there—a hub.

Across the street from the depot was a small, tidy white cottage surrounded by a picket fence, inhabited by a fierce old lady called by everyone in town "Old Lady Buck."

All the kids in town, indeed some of the grownups, were scared of the wild-haired Mrs. Buck, who waved a huge stick yelling menacing curses at passersby. The reclusive old lady owned a swarming horde of tiny white terriers whom I found absolutely adorable. I would lean on the outside of her fence for hours at a time besotted with admiration of her dogs. I talked to them, crooned to them, petted them through the fence. At first Old Lady Buck yelled at me. I stayed very quiet, *never* called her Old Lady Buck, never played tricks on her. I kept coming back many times a day to see her dogs. She could see that I obviously had excellent, discriminating taste in canines so she stopped trying to chase me away. Our mutual dog admiration society was a bond. Mrs. Buck became my new best friend and presented me with my very own gorgeous white terrier, Trixie, the love of my life. I could leave Trixie with her myriad doggie relations at Mrs. Buck's house while I was in school or when we went to

Seattle. The rest of the time, I smuggled Trix illegally into the Moran Apartments. All the teachers knew of this illicit act, but they all loved Trixie, if not me, and never ratted on me.

Once, Mother encountered one of our retired logger friends on Main Street. I heard him confidentially, protectively, telling her that Old Lady Buck had been a notorious Madam of the best red-light house in town during the rip-roarin' lumbering days. I didn't know what a madam was, and it seemed a charming idea to light one's house with costly warm red lights. Surprisingly, even after this steamy revelation, Mother let me continue my relationship with the ex-madam. There was the daily dog exchange with much reporting, conversation, planning. I also ran errands for the old lady. Sometimes I brought her a gift of limp flowers with very short stems which I picked from my "garden." Not only was I the only *child*, I think I was her only *friend*. I never saw anyone else go in or out of that tidy white cottage except the dozens of terriers. Mrs. Buck asked Mother for a picture of me to keep in her parlor. When Mother sent her one of me holding my doll, Mrs. Buck said: "Oh, I'da knowed ya anywhar, but who's that a-holdin' you?"

Behind Mrs. Buck's cottage a high cliff rose all woodsy and wild. My new school chum, Virginia Hill, and I had a secret hideaway ledge up there, inviolately secret because the only egress was through Old Lady Buck's yard. Nobody but nobody but me was ever allowed to go through her yard. I could, however, hold my friend's hand and escort a tremulously frightened girl. Ginny and I named our secret retreat "Paradise Point." We never told anyone about it, except of course, Mrs. Buck, our gate guardian. With a few crackers or a candy bar, we sat there for hours after school or on Saturdays telling stories, fantasizing about the future when we would roll into Arlington in our big limousines, each of us swathed in furs, our alsatians and greyhounds on silver leashes. I also labored, manfully, heroically, to teach tone-deaf Ginny to sing. The long, arduous private lessons which I administered on the ledge were completely unsuccessful. "Deeeeear one, the world is waaaaaiting for the sunrise. Eeeeevery rose is heeeeeeeavy with dew" was our favorite song.

Screech, squeak, squeak, struggle as she would, Virginia could never hit the high note on which I trilled so beautifully. I have a suspicion that she was forbidden to practice singing at home.

One day my mother came home from teaching to find a note from me: "I am sorry I was naughty. I have gone to Paradise, I love you." It covered all bases, but sounded alarmingly suicidal. Since our lair was so secret, Mother had no idea where or what it was and worried for hours until I reappeared, hoarse from singing.

On Saturday afternoons, if we had the required nickel, Virginia, Edna Mae, Betsy and I would go to the rinky-tinky movie house to watch that week's installment of the serial. It was usually either sad or scary, sometimes, deliciously, both. Children were the only at- tendees.

After the movie, going down the street to Mrs. Shoemaker's candy and soda parlor was the very height of delight. The bent-wire chairs and little round tables were our country club. Shoey (I called her that, but I don't think anyone else did) was skinny, red-haired, brusque to most people but a pal of mine from old Royal Hotel days, when I lived across the street from her. Maybe I just gravitated to older red-haired ladies: Mam-Mam, Old Lady Buck, Sugar, Shoey were all older, red-haired best friends. Wasn't I lucky to be *only child* surrounded by such a collection of adoring women?

KATHRYN K. MCNEIL

Trumpet Vine

LENORA PULLED THE STEM of the trumpet vine flower towards her and looked deep down its orange throat. The vine grew inside her kitchen window in the spring and she let it make a pretty frame around it. Seemed like she saw her world through that window during the five years she'd lived there. Standing there, looking out, leaning against the kitchen counter, her mind was far away. Idling, her husband, Hershel, called it. He disliked the way the vine anchored itself to the rock chimney and ran across the roof, like it owned the place.

"Get rid of it, Lenora, or I will," he threatened every so often when he saw her standing there. But she ignored his threats and cooked up his favorite pot of beans and ham hocks for dinner.

Someone told her once, "That plant belongs in Florida, too cold for it here in these mountains." Somehow, it never froze clear down to its roots, and always turned green and peeped out, just when it should, in April, when everything else peeped out in the Smokies.

Florida. Even the name had a pretty sound. Must be a pretty place and different, she thought. Different from the mountains, which was all she ever knew. Come summer, seemed like every other car had a Florida plate. She watched them come and go at the Texaco station that her sister-in-law ran across the highway from her. Some days, there was a steady stream of RVs pulling in for gas. She saw women with pretty blond hair and pretty shoes with tiny straps holding them on looking for the restroom. She often sat on the outside bench of an afternoon, watching the traffic go by, listening to the old men, old retired farmers, comment on the looks of this truck or that, and how poor the new engines were these days, killing the afternoon hours with them till time to go home and cook up Hershel's supper.

"You're lucky, Lenora," her brother, Tom, told her over and over. "You got yourself a home now and a husband who'll take care of you. Why you always mooning about? Remember how it was at the Suttons? That ought to cure you."

How could she forget? Anything was better than her years there. From the time she was fifteen on she took care of babies that arrived each year, cooking from dawn to dusk and in between times. No pay, just board and room. Well, she couldn't afford to be choosy, her parents dying so young and all that. Then Hershel came along and saw her. He wanted a wife was the way he put it, and it was still that way with him. He was older than her by a lot, but he was steady and quiet, and he let her have her way, most times. He worked in his fields from early morning till dinner time, then out again till supper. He liked coming home at the end of the day to a clean house and a pot on the stove cooking his supper, and a young wife to take to bed. She obliged him, but when it was over, and he went off to sleep, she slipped out of bed and sat by the kitchen window and watched the cars flickering by, up and down the highway, wondering where they were going. Always, above them, she saw the deep-black shapes of the mountains, hanging over everything.

Those mountains. Florida folk thought them really special, saying they were nice and cool to be in after living in Tallahassee or Jacksonville. But they weighed her down, kept her cooped up in her little valley, cut her off from things. At night she could see lights high above her in the dark. She'd seen the steep roads the newcomers had cut through thickets of laurel. "So their houses could have a view," they said. Sometimes, she went with Hershel to the high pastures to check on his cows on summer days. Lordy, it was a long way up! And when he drove around a certain bend, the whole world just sat there in front of her. Sitting on a rock waiting for him, looking at all the miles of country she'd never been in stretching out below her, all the coves and ridges and land in between she'd never see, and her valley, Allen's Creek, a thin green shoestring of flat land with misty mountains closing it in, she felt sadder and moodier than ever. She was glad when he was ready to go back down.

She turned away from the window and packed up some bread she'd made to take to Hershel's mother, Alma, who lived across the highway. She didn't much care for Alma, and she knew Alma didn't much care for her. Only natural. Hershel was her only son, after all. Alma sat in the window in her wheelchair all day long, the TV on high, watching the road, watching her, Lenora, too, come and go. Alma even had her big old tulip poplar out in front cut down, so she could see out better. Lenora pulled back her long dark hair and pinned it with a brassy clasp someone left behind in the restroom of the station.

"It's me, Lenora," she yelled, opening the screen door. She knew well and good Alma had watched her walk across the road. It was a habit she had, calling out. An old tom cat jumped off the table and ran out as she entered. Alma had five cats and too much cat fur around for her own good. No wonder she wheezed a lot.

"I suppose you're on your way to wasting time at the store again," Alma said, turning from the window and looking her over.

Lenora had gotten used to those eyes, sharp bright eyes in a wasted old face. They didn't miss much considering how little Alma could move about.

"Brought you some bread for dinner. What you having?" Lenora took the lid off the pot and looked in. "Marcia's fixing you some corn soup?"

"Now you don't need to be snooping around here," her mother-in-law said sharply. "Can't stand people poking their noses in my pots."

Lenora laughed. Alma didn't bother her. She did her duty by her, dropped by each day, tidied up a bit, and then she was free.

Alma's eyes turned back to the TV where a young woman in a low-cut body suit was exercising, strutting up and down, then leaning forward and making circles with her shoulders, her breasts shiny with perspiration. Lenora stared too, wondering why the woman went through such contortions. TV bored her. She'd rather watch real people, strangers who might talk to her. Ask her how she was. What she did. She might not give them very good answers, but she played at what she would say.

"Yes, I live in Allen's Creek near the Texaco Station. You know it? Well, my husband's a tobacco farmer and he owns a lot of land in the valley. We live in a rock house and there's a row of poplars between it and the fields. No, I've no children. I help my husband in the fall, when the tobacco's ready."

Lenora brought herself back from dreaming. "Need anything before I go?" she asked Alma with her hand on the screen door handle.

"Marcia sees to everything I need," her mother-in-law answered, her eyes on the TV. "Go on your way."

The station was quiet, not much going on. It was late afternoon and it was hot. She looked around at the dusty shelves with their gum and hard candies and peanut butter packages that would get a person by on the road without starving to death, and the cold drink box near the door. She'd seen it all every day. It never changed. The old farmers who sat there on the outside bench by the gas pumps had all gone home. She sat herself down and relaxed. A big tractor trailer drove up to the diesel pump. It was snow-white and had blue stripes running across its sides and WE MOVE THE WORLD written in the middle in large letters. She saw the driver jump down from the cab. He looked young and lean in his tight blue jeans. After he had filled up, he sauntered past her, stopped a minute and looked her over, and then went inside. She felt the color come up in her neck.

"Nerve," she thought to herself. "Who does he think he is?" She sat there wondering when he'd come out. Then he was back, standing right in front of her.

"How about a Coke?" he was asking her. "Tastes good on a day like this."

She shook her head.

"Live around these parts?" He tipped back his head and took a long swallow from the can, looking at her sideways.

She thought about how to answer him. The little speech she had prepared for strangers didn't seem right to say now. He must be close to her age. He looked neat, not sweaty and pudgy like so many of the truckers who stopped at the station. "I live over there," and she nodded her head in the direction of her house.

"Pretty around here," he said, looking at the mountains hanging over the valley. "Like it?" he asked her, taking another swallow from the can.

"Not much," she heard herself say. Before she could hold back, she asked, "Where you going?" She had no business asking him that. Shouldn't talk to him at all. Truckers weren't to be trusted, every woman knew that.

"Tennessee, then south to Florida. That's where I'm based. Florida."

Lenora felt her heart pound a little bit. "Hope I get there one of these days," she said, turning away from him. She got up. She felt he was looking at her. Hoped he was.

"Maybe I'll see you again when I come through here next time. Be around?" he called after her.

"Course I'll be around, I live here. Remember?" She tossed her dark hair at him and walked across the highway.

She was flushed and agitated when she got home and slammed the pots around getting supper ready. She must be out of her head talking like that to him. Well, she told him off. He talked to her so easy-like as if she was just sitting there all day, waiting for him to drive up.

The weeks went by and tobacco time was on them. She liked the
hustle that went on now with lots of people around the place, strip-
ping the leaves off the Burley stems, classifying them, carrying them
to Hershel's drying sheds where she and everyone else gathered together to tie them into "hands." Wide, yellow leaves that would
hang in long layers from the rafters to dry for sixteen weeks until
market time. Then she would get to ride in the truck with Hershel
bringing them to Asheville, to the warehouse. Precious as gold, this
harvest load, covered with their own quilts to keep it snug and dry
for the journey. She liked the smells in the dark warehouse where
tobacco from all over the county lay stretched out, golden and
musky, and the growers waiting to hear the price from the lips of the
auctioneer who droned it out, watching for signals from the buyers
in their shirts and ties, waiting to hear that word, "Sold," that sealed
their fate for another year. A good price or one too low, a worrisome
time for everyone who tended the crop all those weeks of growing
and the long months of drying.

It was a sociable time and she cooked steadily. My, how she
cooked. Hams and collards and biscuits and corn on the cob for all
the workers. Everyone was relaxed then, even Hershel. No more
worries about drought or hail or bugs hurting the leaves. The crop
was in safe, and drying in the sheds. One hot afternoon when everyone was winding up the day's work and she had served sweet iced tea
all around, one of the single young men who'd helped them hung
around her, trying to get her to walk outside the shed with him,
away from the others.

"You need a change, Lenora," Joe said. "Walk out with me
where it's cool."

Lenora looked him over hard. She knew his ways. He was handsome and smooth talking.

"Joe Caldwell, I can talk just as easy here," and she leaned
against the corner of the door.

Joe boxed her off from the others with his body and leaned over
and pulled a strand of damp hair off her cheek.

Lenora brushed his hand away impatiently. "You're nothing but a flirt, Joe, and I've no time for you," she said, darting out from under his arm.

But she was secretly pleased he noticed her still. A man could make you feel pretty or the ugliest woman on earth. They had that power. Hershel never noticed what she wore, whether she fixed her hair one way or another. He wasn't one for compliments either, but yesterday he surprised her. He put his arm across her shoulders and said, "Folks are satisfied, Lenora, don't you think?" Well, she knew what side her bread was buttered on. She wasn't dumb, even though Joe Caldwell would like to get her in trouble. She was careful. She'd lead him on, just the tiniest bit, and pull back and act respectable again. Lordy! She'd like to have a man talk sweet to her, tell her a lot of nonsense, make her laugh.

"I've got a new truck, Lenora. We could take a ride, cool off."

Always these offers to break loose hung over her from the young men in the valley. Offers to take a spin, drive fast with the wind blowing her hair back straight, offers to take her somewhere she'd never been.

A week later, she was at the store, sitting outside and wondering if it would rain. Clouds piled up over Purchase Knob and the sky looked dark. Then she saw the white trailer truck with blue stripes drive up. Her heart jumped around inside. Be careful, she told herself.

"Howdy." He stood right in front of her again and smiled down. He had on clean jeans and a snow-white tee-shirt.

"Howdy back," she looked up and had to smile, he looked so nice and fresh. "Didn't expect to see you again."

"Expected you though. Hoped I'd find you sitting here. Coke?"

"No thanks." She watched him out of the corner of her eye go inside and come back with his can. Watch yourself.

"Doing anything this afternoon?" He sat down alongside of her, looking at her.

"Usual. Just waiting till supper time." Her heart was pounding. She should leave. Get up right now and go home.

"Ever ridden in a cab?" He nodded at his truck.

"Never," she shook her head, concentrating on a fly that walked across his leg where his tanned hand rested. It was getting ready to walk over to her skirt.

"Come on then," he said.

She stood up, and as if in a dream, walked over to the truck. He opened the door and helped her in. Then she was sitting high, looking out over everything. He started the motor and they drove out of the station, past her house, past Alma's.

She watched him handling the heavy gears easily.

"Know where you want to go?"

"Florida. Jacksonville, Florida," she said softly.

He looked at her quickly. "That's too far. They'll worry about you."

Lenora shook her head. She felt very calm now. She was going through with this. "That's where I want to go. No one will care."

They drove in silence for a few minutes. "I don't even know your name," he said.

"Lenora."

"Pretty name. Mine's Clem."

"Hello, Clem."

"You married?"

"Yes." She had to say that.

Clem sucked in his breath. "Lenora, I don't want to get messed up in this." He slowed down and pulled over to the shoulder and looked for a turning place.

Lenora felt an awful fear clutch her heart. She didn't care about Hershel worrying. He would do just fine. Besides, she'd be back. The thought of going back now to what was so familiar, to her home, her daily chores, Alma, the station and its old men, made her slightly crazy. She grabbed his arm.

"I have to go to Jacksonville, Florida. I've heard about it. I want to see it bad. I want to walk on the beach and see the ocean. I've never seen nothing but mountains and tobacco." Tears were running down her cheeks. She didn't mean to cry. She brushed them away impatiently.

Clem stared at her. Then he took a clean kerchief from his pocket and gave it to her to dry her eyes. "Running away from home, aren't you? Using me to help you. I thought maybe you liked me."

Lenora took a deep breath to steady herself. Going away for a few days was all she wanted. A change. Then she'd go back.

"Please, Clem? I do like you. You're nice."

He put his hand on her hair, his fingers stroking the long black strands that fell across her shoulders. He was silent. Considering, she guessed. Then he turned back to his wheel and turned on the engine.

"We'll go to Jacksonville, and then you'll go home," he said, putting his truck in gear and moving slowly onto the highway.

They talked a lot as they drove along. Mostly it was Clem talking and she asking questions. There were so many questions.

"What's it like, travelling somewhere different each day?" she asked him.

"It's good. You get tired though, and stiff."

He had such an easy way with her, quiet and friendly, not pushy or grabbing her like Joe would try to do the minute she was alone with him.

"Tell me everything you've seen, Clem." She settled back and closed the window so she wouldn't hear the roar of other trucks passing. She didn't want to miss a word.

Clem told her about Memphis, Tennessee, and the big bridges over the Mississippi. And about how long it took to cross, the river was that big. About the Gulf Coast towns and how pretty they were with the highway and the water close to each other. He told her about Nashville and hearing Grand Ole Opry once. He had rested there and taken in some shows.

"Ever been to Miami Beach?" Lordy, she'd give anything to go there.

"Lenora, you've never seen so many hotels in one place in your life. High ones and flashy signs out in front and people crowding the sidewalks brown as Indians from all the sun-baking they do all day long. Not for me though."

"Why, Clem? I know I'd love Miami Beach." She sighed, thinking about the crowds of people holidaying like it was always Sunday. He looked at her. "Lenora, you'd stick out in a crowd, looking so pretty and natural." He got quiet. "You're going to be in big trouble, you know. You do know that, don't you? Or do you? I declare, girl, I don't think it worries you a bit, what your husband's going to do to you."

She laughed. "He'll get over it. He likes the way I keep his place."

It had gotten dark. Clem drove the truck off the highway towards a flashing light, a huge big coffee cup outlined in neon lights.

"We'll stop here and get some food. Then you're going to call your husband and tell him you're okay, you're just joy riding, and he should come and pick you up." He wrote down a name of a motel for her. "Tell him you'll be at the Seastrand, Jacksonville, and you'll be looking for him tomorrow." Then he gave her some money and showed her where to phone.

She returned before long and sat down across from him in the booth and smiled.

Clem looked at her inquiringly. "Pretty mad?" he asked her. He'd ordered for both of them, ham and grits, fried eggs, and a side order of hash browns. Plus two cups of coffee.

"He didn't say nothing." Lenora picked up her fork. She was hungry. "But then he never does. He'll come for me tomorrow though. He did say that."

"Eat, Lenora. We'll not be stopping again till morning."

She liked the way he just took charge. Clem was kind and good, she decided, and she was lucky. She could care for him.

They ate in silence. When he was through he pushed his chair back and studied her. "Lenora, this is one of the hardest things I've ever had to do. To send you back tomorrow."

They drove all night. She finally dozed off and slid down to rest her head on his knee. Clem reached Jacksonville at dawn, driving through the deserted streets and out to Neptune Beach. He nosed his truck into one of the spaces in the empty parking lot by the fishing pier and turned off the motor. The sun was coming up. He leaned his head back, yawned, and went to sleep.

Lenora opened her eyes. She stared at the dashboard, wonderingly for a moment, and felt the hard leg of a man under her head. She sat up quickly, remembering. The sun hit her in the face, making her squint. She could see nothing but water, hundreds, thousands of miles of flat, sunstruck ocean. She stared at it. Then she opened the door and slipped to the ground. She stepped onto the white sand, mesmerized by the scene before her. The water drew her towards it, across the wide beach until she stood at its very edge, watching the tiny waves lap gently before her and recede, come back to her, and recede again. She kicked off her shoes and waded in, feeling the comfort of it and the sand slipping away beneath her feet as each wave withdrew only to come back again and wash over her toes. Her mind was empty of everything but the water, the lovely, warm, transparent water. As far as she could see there was nothing but ocean and sky. Endless. She threw her head back and laughed. She forgot her valley with its high, heavy mountains pinning her in. She was happy at last. So this was what Florida was like, ocean, sand, and the hot sun making the sea look like blue satin.

She heard the truck door slam and turned to see Clem walking towards her across the beach. She waved at him.

"Clem, it's wonderful!" She walked in deeper, holding her skirt high, between her legs, kicking the water joyously with her feet.

"Never saw anybody like it better than you." He crouched down, sitting on his heels, watching her.

She came out after awhile and sat on the sand beside him. "Thanks Clem." She leaned over and took his warm brown hand in hers and held it against her cheek. "You've treated me special, bringing me here, talking to me, feeding me. Was it dinner or breakfast we ate?" She laughed at him. She felt young and foolish like she might be sixteen again instead of twenty-three.

"Lenora," and he shook his head, "you're too pretty to be

around long without both of us getting into trouble."

"Just a few days, Clem, then you can take me back," she whispered.

"I've got a trip to make, Lenora, across the state today." He stood up and walked down the beach, away from her, like he was thinking a lot about something.

Before he left, Clem fixed her up at the Seastrand right on the beach, and she sat there on the little stoop in front of her room, studying the ocean, letting it soak into her memory. Hershel came and looked at her only once to make sure it was her. He never talked or turned on the radio or stopped, not once, except for gas. He kept his eyes fixed on the road and was silent. She leaned her head back against the seat, trying to remember all the things Clem had told her.

She was home again. Everything seemed the same, just as she had left it. She felt she had been gone for months. She knew she was changed. She felt calmer, more at peace with her lot. At breakfast she made coffee for Hershel, strong and dark the way he liked it. She looked out her kitchen window at the station and the road. She could see them both a lot easier now. Wait. Something was different, missing. Her trumpet vine was gone from the window. She ran outside and looked at the chimney. The vine was gone, cut to the ground. She knelt down, looking at its raw stump, touching the raggedy pith with her fingers. It looked gone for good. A tear ran down her cheek. She brushed it away. She'd make it come back. He'd see. She'd never let him know how bad she missed it. When he wasn't there, she'd water it and feed it, and next spring when everything else peeped out, maybe it would too. He'd see.

She stood up and looked down the highway a long time for a white truck with blue stripes that wasn't there. Slowly, she walked into the house and took out her frying pan to cook Hershel's eggs for his breakfast.

SUSAN RENFREW

Cycle's End

IT WAS 8:20 A.M. and I was trying not to be late for aerobics. I took both grandchildren to school "on time"; the boy at middle school is worried about being late while the girl at high school doesn't want to be early. It means she has to walk to the door through a gang of boys, cigarettes drooping from mouths ready with rude remarks. Parking my car near my class, I noticed the license plate on the big wreck of a car ahead of me. *Wounded in action.* What a strange thing to say about a car. But you could say that about mine. First a woman ran a red light, hitting me broadside, and months later a boy plowed into the back. Then I realized it must not be the car. On the license plate was a small picture of a man's profile that looked like Alexander Hamilton, my favorite Revolutionary character, against a purple shape. Underneath in tiny letters it said "The purple heart." The driver.... Finally, my mind got on track. How sad. He has to put this out for everyone to read because we've forgotten. No one cares all that much anymore. I wonder which war? The car looked ancient, but it might be a 1960s Buick. Buicks used to look heavy and fat like this. He must have been in the Korean War.

Later, I thought about the phrase *wounded in action* as I returned

to the house and started a load of laundry. My old washer was beginning to show its age. In the spin cycle a horrendous banging continued, as if the belt were loose. The thumping sound increased until
the noise became a regular scraping of metal against metal. Still it
continued to run. The clothes were much too damp, but after a second spin cycle they seemed dry enough. I kept using it, knowing it
might stop at any time. Finally, I realized spending money to fix it
would be impractical. Yet it had been a loyal soldier, waging war on
grass stains, crank-shaft grease, pizza sauce drips, and myriad messes
all those years. I had washed baseball uniforms and football pants
caked with mud, the sheets when my daughter entered puberty, and
the long crepe skirts of the tail end of the flower generation. Whenever I felt at loose ends, surrounded by disorder, I would do another
load. There was something comforting in knowing that at least these
clothes would be clean.

Some people smoke to be calm or take walks. I do the laundry,
waging my private battle alone in my wash room, making sure no
time is wasted between spin cycle and dryer, folding clothes into
piles when I wait, never about to empty the counters because the job
of sorting has become much too complicated. Sock after sock waits
for its partner. The jeans which were either my granddaughter's or
daughter's are no longer the problem. Instead, my grandson wears
pants larger than his father's. My task is to find his and then decide
which jeans are theirs. My granddaughter likes hers to fit in strategic
places and my grandson wants them to drop from his waist, but not
plummet to the floor.

Sometimes, I take in a book and sit on the warm dryer while the
clothes turn round and round. Unfortunately, one of my rules is that
I must be doing something useful at all times. Another is that heating the house costs money so never turn on the furnace unless absolutely essential for life to continue. While other rooms may be
freezing, the laundry room is cozy. Poor washer. It was blamed for
those random decisions characterized by a friend as "when in doubt,
you might as well throw in the red socks." I'd had several of those.
Frauke, the German girl who came to help us when my fourth child

was born, had even more. She seemed not to understand about wool's proclivity to shrink when tossed in the washing machine. Once in the back of a cabinet I found a laundry bag filled with my former husband's Brooks Brothers button-down Oxford cloth shirts. He never missed them as he embarked on a new life of customized, imported shirts.

When we were first married, we lived in Fort Sill, Oklahoma, in a little duplex. I took the laundry to an old Indian woman who had three open washing machines in her backyard. Army wives paid her to use those washers while she shuffled around the jiggling machines poking down the clothes with a cut-off broom handle. When the cycles were finished she grunted at us and we would pile up the wet clothes in baskets and take them to a wringer to press out the water by turning an old crank. The water spilled on the parched ground. Then we would carry the baskets home to hang our husbands' khakis on the back line. The weather in Oklahoma was so hot that summer that the clothes at the beginning of the line were dry by the time I put the last clothespin in place. The girl next door brought me over a jar of tarantulas which her husband had caught in our shared backyard one evening. I never hung out the clothes again with the same abandon.

I hated to face the fact that I needed a new washing machine. I felt so close to this one. During my divorce when my life threatened to spin off course, I could feel comforted instead by the steady reliable hum of the washer. We'd seen so much together, so many years. I imagined a TV ad. A gray-haired woman smiles and pats her machine. "My Maytag lasted twenty-five years. It's waged war on dirt for a husband, four children, and now two grandchildren...." (I'd be willing to do a commercial if it paid for a new washer.) That means I will be eighty-six when a new one dies. Who knows what it will be washing then.

That afternoon my brother and I made an expedition to Cherins, an appliance store in the Mission since 1892. For some mysterious reason, he enjoys looking at appliances in case one of his breaks down, and I was glad of his company. Maybe it was nostalgia.

Our grandfather owned furniture and appliance stores in Detroit, which he sold ten years after World War II ended. I worked at the switchboard at his Mack store in the summer of my junior year of high school. I was to answer customers' questions about the time of their delivery, soothe them if they had waited all day, and, as a last resort, transfer the call to Joe, who arranged for the delivery schedule. The salesmen used to hang out in the office behind me, complaining about the false claims of competing stores who ran ads which boasted of living room suites at forty percent off. When the customers rushed in, they were told they had just missed the last set. Perhaps this was why, when the Cherins salesman told us the features of the newest Maytag, I was skeptical. "There's a special tray in the left corner for dispensing bleach, two washing speeds, regular and gentle, and five different settings for water temperature," he explained. I wasn't sure I needed all this, but was intrigued that the machine included a government bond. The store looked like stores from the 1950s with glass partitioned cubicles. Each one had a salesman sitting at a desk loaded with books and invoices who was talking on several different phones at once. Selling appliances seemed to involve so much conversation, but then washing machines that last twenty-five years do limit the potential market.

I purchased a new Maytag and waited for the delivery. All went well until I read *Dump out $15* on the bill. My heart sank. Just to be thrown away, no ceremony, no acknowledgement for all those years of service. I felt low all week. The deliverymen arrived on Wednesday, grumbled about the narrow passage to the laundry room, took the old machine into the kitchen, moved in the shiny white machine, and failed to notice a gray-haired woman, head bowed as the old veteran was rolled out onto the porch and down the steps. Even her soft pats on the enamel lid of the machine as the dolly cleared the hall were not observed. "Thank you," she whispered. "Sorry there aren't taps."

Today, I am at my pastime again. As I walk to the room off the kitchen my granddaughter calls out, "What are you doing, grandmother, bonding with the new washing machine?"

MARGARET GAULT

How to Be Married to a Lawyer and Still Be Happy

MANY YEARS OF MARRIAGE passed in which I tried to have meaningful discussions with my husband, Jim, who is a lawyer. The subjects I brought up were, I felt, of common interest: problems having to do with one of our four children, insufficiency of house-keeping money, decisions having to do with property such as major repairs or changes requiring remodeling or decorating. Somehow, what I wanted to become a discussion—with a consensus at the end on which one of us could act and the other agree—always became an argument. No one ever won the argument; both of us usually were angry by the end of the argument when one or the other stomped out of the room, and, worst of all, action wasn't taken and the problem continued unsolved.

In a flash of insight one wonderful day, it came to me that Jim was a much better arguer than I was. Hadn't he spent three years of intensive study in law school learning everything there was to know about arguing? One of the things they learn, I believe, is that when a premise is posed, it is the bounden duty of a lawyer to test it, question it, argue with it. So the spouse of a lawyer goes through exchanges such as:

"Jim, we really must think about buying a new living room sofa."

"Why?"

"Because this one is completely worn out."

"It doesn't look worn out to me."

"Come over here and sit down. Feel how it sags when you sit there?"

"I like that spot. It's the most comfortable spot on the sofa, I think."

On that wonderful day referred to above, I realized that I could sit on the old sofa for years giving thousands of reasons and each reason would get shot down as soon as I threw it out. The answer lay in changing strategies—no more reasons! If lawyers are so good at rational thought and putting up stone walls of argument as an unconscious reaction due to their training, Jim would never again be presented with the fodder, the weapons, the reasons he so easily turned back when he stymied me. From that day forward, I have omitted reasons in our discussions of important matters in favor of feelings. Lawyers are as illiterate as primitives when it comes to coping with someone else's feelings and rather than try to cope, they capitulate immediately.

"Jim, we really must think about buying a new sofa for the living room."

"Why?"

"I just want one."

"Oh."

"I'm going to the furniture store on Saturday morning to see if I can find one I like. Do you want to come with me?"

"No, anything you like will be fine with me."

Let me suggest a few more expressions of feeling which are absolutely sure-fire in terms of getting you what you want with a minimum of stress and discussion—"It will make me happy" and "It's time."

Yesterday as I began work on this, a doctor's wife told me about one of her most successful strategies. I'm not sure what to call it. Her example was her daughter's cat, who had to be taken in if the

daughter could happily move to New York to take advantage of a
greatly improved work situation. Her husband had said on no condition would he accept that cat into his household. The daughter did
move to New York and on the way to the airport, she dropped off
the cat at her mother's house. When the doctor came home from
the office that evening, he immediately said, "What is that damn cat
doing here?"

My friend said, "What cat?"

BABS WAUGH

Medical School

I THINK THAT I HAVE SPENT much of my adult life trying to atone for dropping out of medical school. My need for atonement is based, not on having taken a place that might have gone to a man, but rather on having been given an unusual opportunity and then squandering it. I know I'm not unique, for many people make false career starts, have unfulfilled dreams. Yet I continue to need to explore this still-painful memory, in the hopes, perhaps, of expunging the pain.

I remember a conversation I had some twenty years ago with my husband, John, when I was approaching fifty. It was a serious discussion, for I was feeling deeply dissatisfied with my life. Our two daughters were grown and I was at loose ends, unhappy, restless, wondering what on earth to do with myself.

"It's just that what I'm doing now doesn't seem to amount to anything," I said.

"Well," he finally said to me, exasperated, "who do you think you are?" I was startled by what his remark implied. Was I really the arrogant creature he suggested? Who did I think I was, indeed? I knew I was living no less useful a life than many of my contemporar-

ies. It was a privileged and active one with a husband I considered
my best friend and two daughters who were self-supporting and living independent, productive lives. Did I feel that I, too, deserved the
kind of respect my husband was enjoying just because I started out
the same way he had? You get that only if you pay your dues, I told
myself, as I studied the floor; you finish your training, you study into
the night so that you can pass your specialty boards, three of them,
each one the first time, as he had, and as you practice medicine
throughout a lifetime, you serve your patients well.

"Well, do you think I'm arrogant?" I asked him.

"Only a little," he replied with a smile.

I was twenty-one when I applied to medical school during the fall of
1948, my senior year at Stanford. Being female helped, for medicine
was one of the earliest professions to lower its barriers to women. I
also looked good on paper; I had good grades, had made Phi Beta
Kappa, and was active in student affairs. I was admitted to four of
the five medical schools to which I applied; Yale turned me down,
though, rejecting me, I decided, because I lost track of my bank balance and my application fee check bounced. Though I didn't think
of it at the time, overcome as I was by jubilation at having four
places offered to me, the Yale dean was perhaps more perceptive
than the others. Did he look for evidence of adequate maturity and
fail to find it? Maybe he was just unhappy about the bounced check
after all.

I chose the University of Pennsylvania and this pleased my father, for he had been worried that I would choose Columbia, which
he considered a "Commie" school. When I arrived at Penn in the
fall, I realized I was no different from the men in my class—happy to
be in, scared, fascinated by the subjects we were to study; from the
beginning we all just did the best we could to survive. Women in
medical school was not a new concept; the class ahead of mine had
three and our class of sixty included seven, a huge and heartening
increase. Though Philadelphia had a women's medical college, none
of us women at Penn had considered it, for we wanted the best for

ourselves, and knew, without much conscious thought, that if we were to enter a man's field, we could level the playing field only by competing on the same terms during our training.

The six other women in my class and I shared a locker room where we left our books and could change into lab clothes. We were friendly, but we never got together socially; I don't think it occurred to us that we might need each other's support.

"How is it being in a class with so many men?" my mother asked when she came to visit me during that first fall.

"Oh, fine," I said. "About half the men talk to us and the other half sort of ignore us. They all call us 'hen medics,' you know." I thought it was funny and so did she.

A Philadelphia aunt lined up a chintz-filled room with ruffled curtains for me in a rooming house near the university, hardly the bohemian medical students' digs I had envisioned. I took my meals at a boardinghouse a few blocks away. Eight or nine Penn students, none of them in medical school, gathered there for breakfast and dinner and together we consumed at each meal, along with conventional boardinghouse fare, two eight-inch stacks of sliced white bread. We must have been ravenous.

After breakfast, I would walk the few blocks to the campus, my load of books and notebooks balanced on my hip, past the diner on the corner we called the Greasy Spoon where we sometimes had lunch, past the Dirty Book Store where, in its grungy interior, we bought our textbooks and lab supplies, across a busy street, and onto a tree-lined path. The University of Pennsylvania campus is set smack in the middle of Philadelphia and is surrounded by noisy, traffic-filled streets. Once on the campus, though, I was in a tree-filled oasis, and as I walked along on those first crisp fall mornings, the falling leaves, new to me, a California native, crunched deliciously under my feet. I would meet other students hurrying to class, and together we would climb the steps of the great gray building that housed the medical school. University Hospital, our ultimate destination, lay behind the medical school and was attached by an underground corridor, but we would have little to do with it during our first two years, for these years were strictly pre-clinical. We studied the human body in health, the first year, and in its diseased state, the second. During the third and fourth years, we would begin to see patients and to apply what we had learned to the diagnosis and treatment of disease.

"You never seem to worry before an exam," a woman in the class ahead of mine said one day as we had a cigarette in the locker room before going in for a midterm. It seems strange now to think of medical students smoking, but almost everyone did in those days.

"Oh, no, I'm frantic," I said, laughing, but I wasn't really. I studied hard and knew when I knew the material; I would sleep well and wake up with a clear head, loving everything about my life then, for I was fascinated by what I was learning, and was doing about as well in medical school as I had in college.

The professors treated the women students with respect. No one told the kind of jokes that would embarrass us, or mixed Playboy pictures of bare-breasted women with their teaching slides as I know was done thirty years later. Perhaps in our day, men were more gentlemanly. Perhaps there were still too few women in the field to threaten them.

A month or so into the fall term, I met John, who was in the class ahead of mine, and soon I spent any extra time I had with him. I was twenty-two when I fell in love with him at an Italian restaurant where the waiter served chianti in raffia-covered bottles and every night an opera-singing flower vendor made his rounds. By Christmas we decided to marry. Sometime that spring, though, we had a conversation that sticks in my memory. We were in his apartment talking about our plans when I suddenly felt that events were moving too fast and that I was in danger of losing something important.

"I'm worried, John," I said, "but I'm not sure I can explain why." I paused for a moment trying to gather my thoughts. "Even though we're married, we'll just go on being who we are, won't we?" I asked him.

"Of course we will," he said, probably not understanding what I meant. I'm not sure I did either. I suppose he managed to reassure me, for we went on to dinner and never talked again about these protean fears. I wish that I had had then the understanding and vocabulary of today. Now, in the nineties, with our collective female consciousness raised by Betty Friedan thirty years ago and by the continuing stream of feminist voices that followed her, I might have given more credence to what I experienced then. I might, too, have given greater value to the opportunity I had. I would have married John in any case, for I was ripe for marriage; I just would have been more wary.

We married in August and I was pregnant by November.

"Tired or careless," was my disgusted sister-in-law's comment when she heard about my pregnancy, for we had planned a trip to Europe with her and her husband the following summer. It was embarrassing. Here we were, medical students who, of all people, should have known something about contraception. We did, of course, but we also thought we knew other important gynecological things—about timing, ovulation, fertile periods, and, most significantly, infertile periods. I missed a period in October, went in to be tested right away, and on a Saturday morning, a week later, received a call from the OB-GYN resident on my case.

"I've got good news for you," he said happily. "The tests show you're pregnant, all right."

"Oh, I see," I said, and he must have heard the flatness in my voice.

"Well, maybe it isn't such good news after all," he said. "Oh, and I need to tell you that unfortunately you are Rh-negative."

John and I were stunned, then excited, then stunned again as we tried to absorb all the implications of our newly discovered condition, and we talked on and on about what to do. Being Rh-negative in those days before blood replacement therapy was possible meant that you could very possibly have only one child, or at the most two. Suddenly the baby I was carrying became our most precious priority.

"I'm not going to have some illiterate maid raise my children," I said, "and besides, we can't afford it." That we couldn't afford help was true in an immediate sense, but supremely false in the longer term. Had I asked my father, he could and would have given us the money we needed to pay for good help. I barely considered the second alternative of borrowing the necessary money for, growing up in the thirties, I had acquired from my Depression-sensitive parents a horror of debt. Besides, my middle-class upbringing had not exposed me to families whose children were brought up by governesses. The option of continuing medical school simply did not occur to me and I had neither the wit nor the imagination to see myriad possibilities open to me.

My parents and John's were ecstatic when we told them the news, and when I told my parents that I would finish the year and then drop out in time to have the baby, my mother didn't say anything at all. Perhaps she was confused by her mixed emotions, her hope for my success as a doctor, overwhelmed by the unexpected advent of a first grandchild. My father then launched into his theory of western civilization, which was that women were truly responsible for its progress because they were the ones who saw to it that children were raised properly, a variation, I see now, of "The hand that rocks the cradle rules the world." Why had he gone along with my desire to go to medical school in the first place? Why had he actually encouraged me, as I believed he had? Why was he willing to pay for my tuition and room and board without a murmur, and yet now was reinforcing the notion that my only option, my duty, really, was to leave school so that I could raise my own children? I see the inconsistency of his message more clearly today than I did then. I don't fully understand my mother's reaction either, for it was she, after all, who had planted the seed for my becoming a doctor. I thought back to an afternoon long ago when I was still a child; I stood by my mother's chair after school and we talked together about what I wanted to be when I grew up.

"I think I'll be a nurse," I said.

"Don't settle for just being a nurse," my mother said. "Why don't you be a doctor instead?" A favorite aphorism of my mother's was "Aim high and believe yourself capable of all things," and she may have said it then. I heard it often enough throughout my childhood.

As I grew up, I took for granted that I would become a doctor someday, but this ambition was always coupled with marriage and children. I would get through medical school, then have children, I thought, though I wasn't quite clear about the timing. At any rate, I would have three or four children, then get back to being a doctor, perhaps when they began school. This last part was too far in the future to worry about.

I wonder now why my mother didn't say just once, during those times when we were talking about my dilemma, "You might think about getting someone to take care of the baby so you don't have to stop your studies," or even, "Maybe you can go back and finish later." I find it remarkable that it was the mother of a fellow female classmate, a surgeon's wife, who tried to warn me of the consequences of my decision. I had never met her but she took the trouble to ask her daughter to pass on her concern.

"My mother thinks you are making a mistake to drop out," she said. "She thinks you should reconsider." If I had made the effort to talk with her face to face, would she have helped me see other possibilities? Why, too, did I not think to seek the counsel of other professional women? Although there were no women professors at Penn at that time, surely there were others in Philadelphia who could have given me some perspective. Perhaps, though, I am asking too much of my former self, for it isn't easy to ask for help when you are young and unsure.

By then, John and I had, without benefit of consultation or counseling, constructed a new path. I would complete the year and drop out, and then have about three weeks to relax and assemble a layette before the baby was due. I made an appointment with the dean to tell him of my plan. As I entered his well-appointed office, he rose from his huge desk to greet me. He was a small, dapper man whom I'd had little to do with. He offered me a chair and sat down again behind his desk, his back to the window, his face in deep shadow. As I began to speak, I watched for his reaction to my embarrassing story. He listened quietly without comment, though I did become aware of a slightly bemused expression on his face, as if he were thinking, this is what you can expect when you let women into medical school. I finished telling him what I planned to do and he gave me no argument at all. He simply listened to what I had to say, accepted my decision, wished me luck and dismissed me.

I wonder now that I even bothered to finish that second year. Did I assume then that I would go back? I really don't know. I do know that I made no grim, midnight promise to myself that I would return, that this was simply a detour on the path to my original goal. Perhaps it was the momentum and rhythm of the school year that carried me through to the summer. Perhaps it was because I loved what I was doing.

I think that John assumed I would go back to medical school sometime and finish; I think that he wanted me to do so. Soon after we got to Ann Arbor for his internship and residency, he broached the subject.

"You really should think about going back now, here in Ann Arbor."

"Oh, but I've forgotten so much," I said.

"It would all come back," he said, "and most of it doesn't matter, anyway."

I simply didn't believe him, and saw myself, ignorant, stumbling, embarrassed, and falling behind my fellow students. Though I didn't believe him then, I know now that he was right. I can see that all the bits of information you learn the first two years get sorted out during the last two years. The pieces of the puzzle come together; you begin to see the big picture. In spite of his urging, I didn't consider going back then. At that point, I had been out of school only a little more than a year, but the same barriers I had seen before continued to seem insurmountable. I became pregnant again that fall, this time on purpose, and then the next spring, I had a baby and a toddler to care for at home. My life was full and pleasurable with other mothers and their toddlers for company during the day and fellow residents and their wives on the weekends. Moreover, I felt that I was doing my duty to my children and husband. I justified my life by thinking that John required a wife at home to tend him, but I think now I did him an injustice. After all, he married me thinking we would be a two-career family, and I know that throughout his career, his attitude toward women in medicine was positive and helpful; more than once he brought woman physicians along into positions of responsibility. Soon, we were looking beyond Ann Arbor to practice—somewhere on the West Coast, in Seattle or San Francisco—and the further away from those first two years I got, the more frightening it seemed to start back.

Some thirty years later, in the eighties, when John and I were having our annual Christmas party for department physicians and residents, I found myself sitting on the raised hearth by the fireplace talking with Margie, the wife of one of John's associates. She was also a doctor, had just had her first child, and was taking some time out from her obstetrical practice.

"I started out in medicine, too," I said. "I think it's wonderful that you plan to go back to it."

"Oh, well," she laughed. "I'm thinking I just might not go back. Taking care of Valerie is so much fun."

"Oh, no, you must," I said, and her husband, who had overheard her last remark, concurred. "You really should get back to it, soon, Margie," he said. "Don't give up now." He moved on to talk with one his colleagues.

"Why did you stop?" she asked me then. A few of the women residents had gathered around us and were listening to our conversation. At least half of John's residents were women, a common thing then, for half the medical students all over the country were women.

"Well," I said, "I married John after my freshman year, immediately got pregnant, and just dropped out after two years to take care of the baby." I could see the puzzlement in their eyes. Why on earth would she do that? they wondered. Why wouldn't she go back?

"Do you have any regrets?" someone else asked.

"Oh, a few," I answered with the cheerful voice I cultivated when I fell into the trap of talking about this part of my past. "You know, it was different in the fifties. It was right after the war, and everyone was staying home and having lots of children. Why, I felt positively barren when I came to San Francisco and had only two." That brought a laugh and then I went on to say, "I've had a wonderful life, but I think what you all are doing is absolutely right. Stay with it." There was a murmur of agreement and then in the pause that followed, someone politely changed the subject.

So what was it in the end? Fear of not measuring up, a misplaced sense of duty and obligation; or was it fundamentally a lack of sufficient zeal? I think the last, though fear and duty undoubtedly played a part. Having a professional career back in the forties and fifties was simply harder for women like myself, women with a certain ability, but with no consuming drive to pioneer, to lead the pack. A few of the men in my class were brilliant and driven, but most were like me, and because they were men whom the world expected to have a career, they proceeded lock-step through medical school, gaining enough knowledge, year by year, to take up their chosen careers and to make their contributions to society. No fits and starts for them. It was as simple as that. Men had to decide how they were going to make a living. Women had to be pioneers.

SUSAN RENFREW

No Regrets?

WHAT DO I REGRET? That's easy to answer right now as I stand at the kitchen sink trying to scrub out the large red marks scattered over my favorite tee-shirt, with a pile of similarly patterned clothes on the counter beside me. I wish I had checked the pocket of Jennie's quilted bathrobe before doing a load of white. I might have found her lipstick, but the assignment is "What do I regret most in my life." Finding the answer is going to be painful. It has to be something I have said or not said, done or not done.

It can be "to mourn the death of" or "to miss poignantly," or "remorse." That captures the feeling for me. "Sorrow for that which is lost or irreparable." "To have distress of mind," or "misgivings concerning...." Not seeing the flowers and birds in Nepal can't be a regret since I can still travel there. Not having an older brother doesn't fit the criteria either. Regret is an intense word.

I won't be the same after my search. What do I regret? Finding this out is like inserting a stick into the well of feelings inside, much as the gas station attendant thrusts the metal rod into the tank to see the level of oil in the engine. Memory is my stick and the pain my gauge.

As I look back over the past, I realize not reading enough to my children is a sorrow. I did read them *The Hobbit.* I'm pleased with that, but nothing much after that. I wish I had shared with them all I knew about art and music, my fondness for cooking. But it is too late. I repeated the same pattern with my grandchildren. I was too busy to sit on their bed and read to them before turning out the light. This brings sadness, but regret is stronger.

What do I regret the most? I was brought up by a subtle method of child raising. My parents were part of an enlightened group of people who did not believe in corporal punishment. I would be sent to my room for certain behavior. Now I don't even remember what I did to have this punishment, but far worse than being kept from seeing people was the look in my mother's eyes. Doing whatever it was I did meant to her that I didn't love her. An article I read as an adult explained that Americans tend to use this type of parental control while Europeans followed a different practice that said, "Do it because I say so and get a whack if you don't." Harsh as this seems and certainly, the evidence for child abuse in this country is enormous, I wonder if that European method wasn't cleaner. Words of a Tina Turner song come to mind, "What's love got to do with it?"

I grew up feeling any time I disagreed or was thoughtless, I hurt my parents and especially, my mother. I brought this attitude to school, in an all-girls country day school where I graduated in 1949. Most of my teachers did not appreciate students challenging their ideas. We were to feed them back what they taught us. I included what I had learned at home, that if I argued with them it showed I did not like them. I grew to hide what I thought, afraid I would hurt their feelings if I disagreed.

Another element entered this picture when I was twelve. I remember having a heated discussion with a boy named Dan Chestnut in the car, when Mother was driving us to the ice-skating rink. After he got out, she turned to me and said sadly, "Boys will never like you if you argue with them." It was a shock then. Behind it, I read that I wasn't all right as I was. I needed to hold myself in check.

But as I look back to see what I regret, a very surprising thing happens. I don't regret the times I have been angry and spoken my piece or the times I have said what I thought, especially if it meant defending someone against what I felt was unjust, not even the times when I was mistaken in what I thought. I regret those times when I didn't say anything. I regret sitting on my feelings in order to make relationships harmonious. My mother's unconscious assumption that I didn't love her if I did certain things affected my relationship with others. Disagreeing in the right way can help some new attitude to emerge.

When I was twenty-two, married, and teaching second grade in a large grammar school, Frank Gagliardi, a little boy in my class, broke his arm on the playground. His parents were notified and in a short time his mother and father, a powerfully built man who worked in the smelting furnace of the local automobile plant, arrived. They did not tend to Frank. He looked like a small replica of his father, a smaller wedge with strong shoulders and a commanding personality who could yell "hit the dirt" during a game of war on the playground and have the entire group of children fall on the ground. His mother rushed to the kindergarten to see how her daughter was. She had sent her to school that morning with a high fever and the father stormed down the hall to the principal's office to chew him out. I stayed with Frank trying to comfort him, but as the minutes ticked by and I watched his face pale and almost turn green, I felt furious. Ordinarily, I was reluctant to confront the principal or disagree with parents, but this time, I left Frank, tore down the hall and burst into the office. "Talk about this some other time. Frank needs to see a doctor immediately. His arm is broken." The hostile father yelled, "He's my son. I'll do what I want." I slammed the door and returned to my classroom, furious at the parents, at the principal, at life, and sat at my desk unable to even look at Frank. Soon they came to get him and the next day, the father stood at my door willing to apologize.

Another time, a group wanted to start a docent program at a local museum. The main organizer of the plan addressed a large audience to promote her program. One of her tactics was to say two of the curators were not helpful. I knew them very well and suddenly found myself standing and disagreeing with her, saying they were retiring within the month and certainly would have helped if they were in a different situation. Others criticized me for speaking out, but I was never sorry.

What I do regret are the times I did not speak out. I remember the time my eighteen-month-old daughter fell against an ear swab while I was changing her diaper and lacerated her ear canal. The doctor, a cocky little man, told her she was a bad girl for hurting her ear and when he told me to step out of his office because seeing me made her cry more, I did. I should have gathered her into my arms, told him off, and left his office. Or I remember the time when I had a hemorrhoidal blood clot after my son Todd's delivery and was back two days later in the hospital emergency room with my gynecologist, who told the nurse this procedure was much more painful than labor. He had had a similar problem. Only a man would make a remark like that. She acted surprised, but didn't say anything nor did I. Instead, I made sure I took appointments when his partner was the only one in the office. I let women down when I didn't argue with his assumption, and I did not give him the chance to change his perception.

There are things I regret which aren't connected to speaking my mind. They are things I wish I had done differently. I will always wish I had taken our old Great Pyrenees, Thistle, to the vet's a day earlier. She had cut her paw, exploring a neighbor's backyard, and I thought her licking would help heal the wound and I didn't want her to be hurt by the veterinarian. Also, at that time in my life I was worried about the cost. As it turned out, her foot was infected and needed to be amputated. When I had to make a decision about what to do, a woman doctor asked, "What is the quality of her life?" I thought of how she slept most of the day, lying so still that I thought she had died. Food did not interest her. Her only joy was rummaging in backyards. I decided to have her put to sleep and then wept with regret for not bringing her sooner. The kind doctor led me down a corridor to a back door so I did not need to walk through the waiting room in tears. Now I wish I had stayed with Thistle until the end.

Another memory brings regret. I will always ache when I think of my second son, Todd, when he was fifteen calling me from the basement, and my assuming he was just trying to get me to do one more thing and didn't run right down the stairs. When I did, I found him with a broken bone in his foot. He had been lifting weights and lost his hold of the bar.

One of the definitions of regret is something irreparable. In a way, that is true. The past can't be changed, yet in doing this recounting, I have found I can foresee what I might regret if I don't do or say something now. That is a gift.

MARGARET GAULT

A Boys' Mother

JUNE, 1995—A BEAUTIFUL early summer day in a house on the Tiburon shore of San Francisco Bay. The Parachutists Reading Group was assembled for its last meeting of the September to June year. Luncheon was served and our leader, J.J. Wilson, had brought her sister to be the featured speaker. As we balanced the luncheon plates on our knees and ate the delicious offerings of this crowd of skilled, experienced, and generous cooks, laughter bounced off the living room walls and the buzz of good friends' conversation filled the room.

Suddenly there was a gap in the noise, as often mysteriously happens in a group, and I heard J.J. from across the room say to her neighbor, "You don't suppose she wears nail polish, do you? I don't imagine anyone in this group wears nail polish. I certainly hope not anyway."

Horrified, I looked around the room. There were twenty to twenty-five women of a certain age clustered there but it is a large room and I could see everyone, even everyone's hands. One by one, I quietly stared at the hands of women I have known, some for as long as thirty-seven years. Not one was wearing nail polish. Perhaps

there was a smidgeon of colorless Cutex hurriedly applied on one or
two, but not one hand showed the evidence of weekly manicures or
carefully chosen color to harmonize with the outfit or the lipstick. I
could scarcely believe my eyes. The evidence was overwhelming.
The years had brought me to a state I would have fought against
with all my being had I only realized what was happening. Had I become A Boys' Mother?

Most families develop secret language and jokes to communicate
ideas in shorthand, and my family was no exception, particularly my
mother, my sister, and I. One of our secret epithets was the term,
"boys' mother," to indicate a certain kind of woman. The fact that
most of the women who fit the category were the mothers of boys
inspired the classification. Boys' mothers had no one to tell them
that their slips showed nor that their lipstick clashed with their
sweaters nor even that they had lipstick on their teeth. They had no
one to discuss hair styles with nor skirt lengths. No one notified
them if they made an effort to look nice, such as polishing their fin-
gernails or wearing earrings that matched their eyes. As for what to
wear to a special event or which blouse goes best with which skirt,
forget it. No one cared. The boys' mother syndrome arose out of
this situation as a defense. The boys' mother chose simplicity as the
only way out. Neatness and cleanliness counted. Otherwise, she
chose the safe route to travel. Her skirts stayed the same length, her
nails stayed unvarnished, her hair was always the same, save for the
routine trim; a simple style, short, usually straight, often mannish.
Her colors were neutral, her dress styles so classic that they never
had to change. She must have bought new clothes now and then but
it was never apparent. Her heels were low, her shoes laced, and her
stockings did not gleam as silk or later, nylon, stockings do. Her
stockings were guaranteed not to run very often. Jewelry was not in
evidence unless grandmother's lavaliere came out for a black-tie occasion. The demeanor was pretty serious and the movements
brusque and purposeful.

We three, mother, my sister, and I, spent hours commiserating
over the fate of those poor women. How much they missed! It

seems, looking back, that we three spent as much time mulling over feminine subjects and concerns as children today spend watching television. It was so much fun. The most delicious laughter often stemmed from a consideration of somebody else's horrible taste or miserable mistakes in choosing the suitability of an outfit or accessory. What did we learn from this? We absorbed values that had to do with trying to look attractive at all times, spending a lot of time on appearance, style, and panache. What happened to me? After high school, I left home, met a lot of people from New England who considered it was perfectly okay to wear a beige sweater with a gray skirt. Then I got married and had three boys, although God in His infinite mercy gave me a daughter too. As the realization swept over me at Kathy Johnson's house last June that I was well and truly a boys' mother, I resolved to change. Five months have gone by. As I type, I stare at my unpolished nails, unkempt cuticles and hangnails. I have betrayed my heritage and my mother's teaching. Perhaps it's too late to try to change.

My sister had two daughters and no sons. She looks great and her nail polish is never even chipped.

JEAN-LOUISE N. THACHER

A Memoir of Mother Teresa

AS USUAL, DECEMBER 10, 1992, I was trying to crowd too many things into one day, and was late arriving at St. Paul's Church in San Francisco. The church was jammed for the ceremony, the taking of the intermediate vows of the novices of the Missionaries of Charity. I walked along the left of the altar. Surely this was the door Mother would enter.

I longed to greet her in the Indian manner. Hands, palms together, touching my forehead, head bent, and then see Mother's beautiful smile of recognition. Our friendship goes back a very long way to Calcutta in 1950. Mother was the subject of some publicity then because Pope John XXIII had just given his permission for the foundation of her new congregation to be called the Missionaries of Charity.

Calcutta needed Mother Teresa. It was a place with monumental human problems. Bubonic plague and cholera were in epidemic form. It was crowded with refugees, Hindus from Pakistan filled the streets and pushed the sacred cows out of the way to eat from the garbage cans. The homeless filled the railroad stations, sleeping on the floor to keep cool and escape the sun. They lined up to fill their pails with water from a single faucet. They had to sleep in the water line for it often took twelve hours to reach the faucet. There were people who died waiting. The bodies lay there until the trashmen came. The proper way to dispose of a dead Hindu is cremation on the banks of a river, preferably the Ganges. In Calcutta, wood was very short and very expensive. The favorite fuel was dried cowdung. For the wealthy, huge bonfires were built and the widow often committed *suttee* (suicide) by throwing herself on her husband's funeral pyre. With all the refugees, often the municipality had to hold mass cremations. No one knew who had died or where they had come from. The poor had nothing to look forward to. It was a distressing place to live. Calcutta was full of dirt, misery, disease, and tragedy. A difficult post for my husband as Consul at the American Consulate. He had just completed language school, spoke Hindi, and was in charge of the political section.

Though five months pregnant with our first child, I had chosen to be with my husband rather than giving birth in San Francisco or Washington. I thought my husband was more important than any doctor and couldn't visualize what I had been told about Calcutta. Here I was in a world that was not only frightening but appalling, and which I could neither escape nor ignore nor do anything about. I was sure I was going to die in this cauldron of humanity. I would sit on the veranda of our third-floor apartment and look out over the tidy garden with the hand-clipped lawn and the blooming cannas and the bougainvillea and flame-of-the-forest tree. Beyond the tree was a brick wall topped with rows of broken glass glittering in the sun and then the street.

There was a huge garbage can opposite the iron gate of the compound where the guard always stood. Some kind of cattle always seemed to have its head in the can. Beside the can was a dark, skinny Indian, all angles, and clad only in a white loincloth. He seemed to be made of dark sticks as he leaned against the can waiting for his turn. He paid no attention to the wild, filthy pye dogs who sniffed at him and trotted on. Leaning against the pink house wall was a slender woman in a filthy sari holding an emaciated baby to her dry breast.

Squawking crows flew low over the garbage can and dove shrieking towards the bull's head in the mouth of the can and the hands of the beggar. The sun was hidden in the hot greasy sky by the gray smoke from the dung fires and the moist heat of the air. Calcutta had ninety-five percent humidity, which went a long way in explaining the rampant sickness and disease. Covered with black mold, moss, and dirt, even the building looked sick.

I would sit on the porch wondering what on earth I was doing bringing another human being into this place to be loved and cherished and require so much of the limited facilities. This was a baby we had longed and waited for, and now I worried for its survival. Somehow it didn't seem right to be sitting under a great ceiling fan and drinking afternoon tea served by a white-uniformed, barefoot bearer. Francis not only poured the tea but served me fragrant, freshly baked gingerbread cookies. I really couldn't enjoy the service. It didn't help to turn my back on the garden.

One night at a dinner party, I saw an Indian lady who was on the YWCA board with me. It was a very hot night, dinner was interminable. I was feeling very fat, puffy, swollen, and bored.

"Shuda," I said, "Why doesn't the municipality do something about all the people in the streets? We can't even walk outside our door without someone asking for something." Usually I was too diplomatic to bring up such unpleasant subjects at a party.

"No money," said Shuda. "No *floos* (money), too many people."

"But surely they can go some place. Be taken somewhere...." I paused hopefully.

"Bini," Shuda looked at me thoughtfully. "Bini, there's a nun, she was born in Yugoslavia of Albanian parents. She is trying—" Shuda looked hard at me, at my swollen stomach, the sweat pouring down my face, at my feet swollen below the elastic stockings I had to wear.

"What is her name? I would like to meet her. Where is she?" Shuda then looked away. "Maybe after, maybe after—" I must have looked very disappointed.

"Yes, Bini, yes, after the baby."

Because of many frightening complications the birth turned out to be longer than anticipated. Finally, it was right for Shuda to take me to see Mother Teresa.

The first location of the Missionaries of Charity was in the depths of Calcutta. Our driver Mohammed didn't want to take me there and kept muttering at Shuda in irritable Bengali. I told him firmly to follow directions. Finally we drew up in front of a dirty mildewed wall that had once been orange.

Through the iron gate there was a brick courtyard with grass trying to grow between the uneven bricks. A small woman in a white sari with a blue border came out one door and threw a bucket of filthy water into the sewer and started in another door. She was dressed like our baby's *ayah*. Shuda called to her.

"Mother," she said, "Mother, this is Bini, she's American. She wants to see what you do."

I did *namaste* (the traditional Hindu greeting). Mother returned my greeting and then led us into the great house. I had been a Red Cross aide. I had worked in military hospitals as a psychiatric social worker. I worked in the Civil Hospital in Pakistan right after partition; I had even bought meat in the open-air market in Karachi with crows and flies flying and cats and dogs underfoot and the meat carcasses hanging in open air on great copper hooks and the lepers begging and wailing and waving their fingerless arms, but nothing had prepared me for this scene.

The huge room was without partitions; the black iron cots were all full of scantily covered men and women. They were moaning and groaning as they lay on their single-sheeted cots mostly without pillows. Moving about them were a few young nuns about seventeen or eighteen years old, former students of Mother's at St. Mary's High School in Calcutta.

They were carrying water, sponging faces, offering tea, one was holding the hand of a gaunt man and leaning close to his face to hear his words. There were suppurating wounds over which flies were crowding on arms and legs. There was a tiny dead baby with eyes staring at the ceiling. One man was looking at his right hand with four missing fingers. In a few seconds, I had seen, smelled, and heard enough. Here was someone who was doing something. It certainly wasn't enough, but it was something. I muttered about having to nurse my baby and we left. Mother very politely invited us to tea. I was afraid I might be sick.

Back in the car, I asked Shuda what we could do. She studied my face. Then she answered slowly:

"For you, give money." When I got home, before I touched my son, I took a shower, washed my hair, and completely changed my clothes.

The American Women's Club of Calcutta was holding its annual fund-raising bazaar. For some reason I was in charge of the bingo game. It certainly was better than being in charge of the bake sale or the cafeteria or the homemade goods. It wasn't much work and really rather fun calling the numbers and being part of the excitement. We made lots of money.

The Welfare Committee of the Women's Club was in charge of deciding where the money should go and asked for suggestions from the members. I wrote a strong letter in favor of Mother Teresa and the Missionaries of Charity. I received a negative answer, which gave me the option of presenting my case before the committee. This I did and could hardly believe my fellow Americans. They turned down the whole proposition; they refused to visit the Missionaries and insisted over and over that: "Giving money to Mother Teresa was like pouring it down a Calcutta sewer. We would never see any positive results."

I left the meeting shaking and in tears. I couldn't believe it. I kept thinking of all the things I could have said, but if I had said them, I don't think I would have left with any dignity at all.

When my husband came home, I inquired carefully about the state of our finances. With greatest care and caution, he felt we could give Mother one hundred dollars. Then I really sobbed. This was a lot of money. Mother hadn't asked for it, but it was close to what she should have gotten from the Women's Club. After that, every Tuesday morning I went down and worked with Mother Teresa from nine to one.

I have to admit that I did not work in the Nirmal Hirady Home for dying destitutes. I think Mother was afraid I couldn't stand it. I did work in the combined school and hospital for children. Often I helped the doctor change dressings and splints and then gave backrubs and massages. I bathed the children in their beds and sang American folk songs since none of us spoke the same language. Sometimes at the end of my duties Mother would invite me for tea. This was a great opportunity to learn about the order. Most of what she told me is now public knowledge; while riding on the train to Darjeeling on her way to a retreat, she received the call to leave the convent and help the poor. In order to answer this call within her, she had to write to Pope John XXIII. By return mail she received permission to be an unenclosed nun. She took an intensive nursing course, returned to Calcutta, and left the beautiful Loreto Convent for a shed that was given to her in the slums. She started her school and her orphanage in 1950. Here I worked with her. In early 1952 she received a new home for the Dying Destitute out near Kalighat Temple on the Hoogly River.

One day she came to me in the orphanage. She was quite excited because it looked as if she could rent a place in the deepest part of the slums for a dispensary for treatment of lepers. She explained that if treated early enough, leprosy would not develop. There were some remarkable new pills for its treatment. She wondered if my car and driver were outside. Mohammed was always there. Those were my husband's orders, not to leave me alone in this poor and dirty part of town.

We got in the car and proceeded down the narrow dirty streets that were becoming familiar to me. We arrived at the place where Mother hoped to rent facilities, only to be told that the neighbors had heard about the clinic and would not permit it in their neighborhood. Mother talked with their leaders but it was no use.

As we drove home, I patted Mother's hand in sympathy. I was trying to comfort her. She had been looking for a clinic for a long time. She turned to me angrily for my lack of faith that the Lord could solve the problem and said, "The Lord will provide." Such was her faith! How could I be in doubt? When we got back to the mission, Mother asked me in to tea. I couldn't seem to come up with any light chatter. Then the phone rang. The way Mother greeted Dr. Senn, I knew he was someone special. The Bengali was too fast for me to follow, but the message had to be wonderful.

Dr. Senn was a well-known leper specialist and had phoned Mother to tell her that he was retiring and wanted to devote his life to God by starting a leper clinic and hospital. I started crying and Mother went to the chapel to pray.

Often at the end of the morning, we would have tea together. I would hear her problems and her joys, but mostly I began to appreciate and understand her love. In the course of the year, I learned the vows of poverty, chastity, obedience, and charity that she lived every day as she served the poorest of the poor.

She told me once about leaving the convent where she was teaching, carrying only five rupees (about seventy cents). As she left the convent, she gave four rupees to a poor lady she saw on the street. Then a priest came to her and asked for a rupee. She hesitated; this was her last rupee and she had no idea where her next was coming from, but she gave it. That afternoon, the priest found her again and handed her an envelope. It contained fifty rupees which the priest said a rich man had given him for her work. "So now, God had begun to bless my work," she said and smiled.

By the time we had to leave Calcutta, I had interested several American women and one British lady in working with Mother Teresa. At our last tea together, I was delighted to learn a wealthy Indian gentleman had promised to send four qualified nuns through medical school. Mother was permitted free passage on trams by the Bengal government. A wealthy Indian gave her a limousine and driver to pick up the dying from the streets. (She always took them to the hospital first, but most of them ended up at Nirmal Hirady.)

I was thinking of her beautiful smile, when the organ started playing and the procession into the church began. Mother marched down the center aisle behind the Archbishop of San Francisco and his mitre bearers and assistants. She was at the end of the procession, shivering in her thin blue-and-white sari with her shoulders hunched and her step as firm as ever. I wanted to throw a cashmere shawl over her shoulders.

The service was brief, the prayers and vows were beautiful. In the middle I remembered the last part of the story of the nuns who went to medical school. They returned to the convent and began requesting all sorts of sophisticated equipment for the patients. They wanted an iron lung, a complete lab, an X-ray machine, etc., etc. Mother responded simply that her work was with the poorest of the poor and she couldn't afford such equipment. Since they would not be happy without it, they should work in the Calcutta hospital where the equipment was available. That was the end of the sophisticated medical unit of the Missionaries of Charity.

As I watched the ceremony, it seemed there was a special glow about Mother. Near the end they said my favorite prayer.

"Make us worthy, Lord, to serve our fellow man throughout the world who live and die in poverty and hunger. Give them through our hands this day their daily bread and by our understanding love give peace and joy."*

While the procession moved towards the door, I remembered two other of Mother's sayings. The first was that the biggest disease today is not leprosy, cancer, or tuberculosis, but rather the feeling of being unwanted, uncared for, deserted by everybody. The other was: "Politicians should spend more time on their knees," and my favorite, "Men need silence." Alas, Mother was whisked away in a marvelous limousine. I couldn't reach her but was blessed for having seen her.

*Something Beautiful for God: Mother Teresa of Calcutta, Malcolm Muggeridge. Image Books, 1977. Page 30.

Grandchildren

SUSAN RENFREW

Ebb and Flow

I NO LONGER MAKE MOUSSAKA with David. He will be
fifteen in December. He surfs instead. He calls Wise Surf Shop for
the "wave report" and if it's good I drive him thirty minutes to
Pacifica, his surfboard carefully placed so the vulnerable sharp
"prow" sticks out into the front seat between us. We follow the coast
where the renovated beach paths and highway edge the ocean. We
choose this route because he likes to watch the waves. And I am
learning how to judge them.

"Gramma," he said, his blue eyes gleaming. "You can tell when
the surf is good. See how glassy the water is? Look at the size of the
swells. See that. There's a good ground swell."

"What else do you look for?"

"I see how long it is between the sets and whether there is a
steep, long wall, and I watch for the sections to see how long the
ride will be."

In the beginning, I worried about his surfing. Usually, he went
alone. I took a book along and waited for him on the beach, but I
soon found he wanted to surf for hours and it was impossible to get
his attention from the shore when my back hurt from sitting too

long. It was hard to see where he was. I would be watching one group of black rubber-suited figures floating on the surf like a block of sea birds and then discover he was in another group further away.

When it was too chilly to sit on the beach, I sat in the car working on a seminar I would lead in a few weeks. At first, I loved it. No phone. No temptation to fix a cup of tea, no chance to do one more load of laundry. I had to study. When my feet got cold, I just turned on the heater for a brief warm-up. The easiest place to park was near the outside shower. Surfers used the hard spray to clean their wetsuits and then stripped to bathing suits to wash off the salt water. Sitting in my cozy car, I wondered how they could stand the cold water after being out in the water all day. It brought back the years when my three sons were still in high school. All those male bodies filled with energy, bumping each other, flexing muscles, sharing a quick moment. This was a perfect spot for a life-drawing class. No two shapes were the same. Most of the surfers were boys, but men came too in the later afternoon and a few athletic girls.

I soon learned that David and I had to set a time for his day's surfing to end. He could stay out in the surf six hours at a stretch and I found it difficult to stay three. I knew by then that I could never swim out to save him, nor could I yell loudly enough for other surfers to hear over the crash of the sea.

He assured me, "Surfers look out for each other. Besides, I would never surf if no one else was there."

Another time, he explained, "Wetsuits float."

And finally, I accept what his mother and I both knew—that boys need to risk in that journey from child to man. We devised a plan. He would call at the Taco Bell down the beach when he was ready to come home and either his mother or I would pick him up, but sometimes the phone was out of order. One evening, when he hadn't called by six, I was frantic though his mother was sure he'd gotten a ride with someone else. I left dinner cooking on the stove and drove the thirty minutes to the beach at Linda Mar and waited on the shore while the final surfers caught the waves until the sun set and the moon rose. I called home. He wasn't there. It was eight o'clock. The sky was now an inky black. Not a single surfer crossed the wake of a phosphorescent wave.

Tragedies happen just like this. A beautiful night, a sense of there being meaning in the universe and then.... I tried not to think of the consequences. Other mothers had waited for sons, other grandmothers. The widow walks high above the roofs of Victorian houses in the East attested to that. I called home again. He was there.

His interest in surfing began with his Uncle Todd, my third child, who moved to Pacifica because it was near the water, allowing him to come back from work and catch a wave or two. But it was in David's bones from his father, who spent his high school years in Hawaii on a long board riding the surf. When I first visited my daughter and new son-in-law in Kauai, I used to watch his father sitting on his haunches on a rise above the white sandy beach, waiting for the surf to change. "He's so patient," I thought. "And so observant. He knows just when a pattern shifts signaling the beginning of good waves." He'd wait for hours and then suddenly run with his heavy board down to the water's edge and ride it out, pumping with his strong arms in sure, quick strokes.

Now seventeen years later, I enjoyed driving along Ocean Beach seeing the newly planted grasses take hold. David and I followed the flat sweep of highway and then swooped down into Pacifica from the high cliffs where the hang gliders set out. At first, David surfed alone. No other friends were eager to stay out for hours in that cold water, but eventually, Victor joined him with his small foam body board. Again, I worried about taking an inexperienced boy out to the beach, but Suko, his mother, assured me he was a good swimmer. "David is such a good athlete and he'll take good care of Victor." She was right. Victor was one of my favorites. He never walked when he could run, his small thin legs scurried along at a tireless pace. It was Victor who would greet me with a "Hi, Sue. What's up?" He was also the peacemaker, feeling everyone's problems rested on his shoulders.

"Just like you, Gram," David observed.

He then explained. "Did you see how he approaches the waves? He'll be good, Gram. He has patience and he's willing to risk."

Even though David loved to go out beyond the cresting waves, he stayed near shore to be there if Victor needed him.

Preteen boys are delicious company. David and I were good friends sharing thoughts on our trips back and forth to the beach. I told him how I felt about people and one day he patted my hand affectionately and said, "Oh, Gramma, you are always for the underdog." I felt accepted and not judged.

He told me about his fear of sharks and how it felt when something bumped him under the water. He would lie on his board not letting any part of his body hang over the side, and count to ten to get his courage back and then start out again. I used to feel that way about letting my arms or legs hang over the side of my bed at night when I was small. Whatever that creature was under there, he couldn't get me.

When he and his seventeen-year-old sister weren't speaking, we talked about that and why he felt he needed a combination lock on his door. He wished his father could be with him more, but understood how his work kept him so late, and with this he would tell me the role a father should have and what he hoped he would do.

Once he confided that he didn't think we went to heaven when we died, not at first, but to some other planet where we had a chance to make up for our mistakes or to a planet on a higher level if we'd lived well. I asked when he'd thought of this and he replied, "When I'm out there on the water, I wonder about things."

He had changed so much since he was little. When he was two and camping with his family in the Sierra, he'd gotten up early and wandered around in his PJs and bare feet. Before anyone had thought clearly, he ran to retrieve a plastic football just over the spot where the campfire had been the night before and burned the bottom of both feet on smoldering coals. His family drove the agonizing one hundred miles-an-hour trip down from the mountains, refused by one hospital after another because they were not equipped to handle severe burns, until they were told to try the Burn Center at St. Francis Hospital. The weeks there were etched in his memory for years. He remembered the little retarded girl who'd pulled her mother's coffee cup over on herself, the mechanic whose drill exploded, and the lady in the white coat who had him draw pictures of where it hurt. He recalled how his grandfather brought him a little red wagon so he could be pulled around the ward. From then on he was cautious and needed to be near his mother. Relatives called him "mamma's boy" and shook their heads. But in time, he ventured farther a little, gradually trusting other people.

Since his family and I lived in the same house, he and I were often together. When he was ten he helped me fix layers of eggplant, tomato, and hamburger meat for a moussaka or sat in the kitchen just to talk. But lately, we have been in the period people warn about when boys find it difficult to say hello and communicate instead in grunts and monosyllables. All your foibles which they found endearing at ten become impossible to stomach at fourteen.

"I'm glad I'm not like you, Gramma." We had just passed a couple and I was wondering out loud who they were, where they were going, if they loved each other. "You get in everyone's business." If I said anything I believed strongly he'd hold his ears. "Don't yell, Grandmother."

I've always known mornings are not his thing. But in this dark period, he walked around the house before school with his neck rigid, barely able to answer with a one-liner to my questions. The immobile head, I finally figured out, was to keep his wavy brown hair in place. The style, a euphemism, is to wear very long hair plastered on top with shaved sides. To keep the top hair from falling into the eyes, you move your head as little as possible until the hair spray sets. I learned about the pants too large for his father long before. This had started with MC Hammer's dance routine to rap music and now, though this Oakland rap star is passé, his style lingers on.

We stopped having philosophic conversations about life and death. If I reached out to give him a hug, he turned away. His frequent comments to me were "got a problem" or when I did something or asked something he considered foolish, he'd say, "Welcome to the twentieth century." It brought back my son's remark, "Earth to Mom."

I'd been through all this twenty years ago. We had few talks at all without his looking as if I were deaf when I asked the same question he'd mumbled the answer to three times already. This was a dreary time when I seriously wondered if the former close feeling hadn't been a figment of my imagination.

We argued. We tried silence. In one horrible encounter at the Price Club, he told me it didn't matter what I bought, I didn't cook anyway. And teary, I told him all the way home that he had been cruel, that I loved to cook, but no one tried to taste anything new. That it killed my enthusiasm for trying different recipes. And when he just sat there not looking at me, I told him, "That just isn't what you tell someone if you really want them to fix dinners for you. You encourage them. And if you hurt them you say, I'm sorry."

I felt if I failed to explain a better way for him to express his point of view, future "womankind" would suffer, and at the same time, I could see how men withdraw from women's sudden emotional response, not expecting it and not knowing what to do or say. I had no idea at the time why his remark brought my tears. Now I see I was crying for a lost relationship.

We continued to make our trips to Pacifica, but they were silent ones. "Your music gives me a headache. All those violins." And his gave me one. And then one wonderful day he burst out, "Cool."

He was sitting in the front seat of the car only in shorts, with one arm draped over his head and his nose turned toward his shoulder.

"Cool, Gramma," he said again. "I have armpit hairs."

Soon after that he showed me how he had "six packs," which he explained are the three sets of muscles men can have on their chest. I never realized before that it was physically possible to have the chest and stomach of a Japanese temple guardian with his defined mounds of hard muscle. He asked me to punch him as hard as I could to show how strong he was, shades of his Uncle Todd, who still asks me to slug him in the stomach and then gloats when I hit his "stone wall." Every few days, David tries out his height against mine, and weekly he seems to grow. I no longer know who is answering the phone. "Is there some new man in the house?"

Now instead of patting my hand and agreeing with what I say, he has a new gesture. He pulls an imaginary cable car chain and says, "Yeah" in a deep voice. His favorite trick is to pick me up and twirl me around until I beg to be put down.

He describes surfing as we drive. "Gram, you know those seals with spots at the aquarium? Sometimes I am out in the water and feel as if I'm being watched and then I see all these little monks looking at me with dark, moist eyes. You should be there when the pelicans fly overhead. Suddenly one of them folds his wings and dive bombs into the water and then others crash after him. They are as big as I am. I think they're my favorite."

"I love them too. Ever since their shells were found to be too soft-shelled from pesticides, I've worried about them."

"There you go again, trying to protect everyone." He grinned.

I trust that this was the end of our months "apart" and risked asking, "What is it about surfing that you especially like?"

"You get so much respect for nature. You are in the womb of the earth." I grabbed a pencil and wrote what he said on a lid of a box I had beside me, afraid I would forget his exact words.

"Nothing else in my life I've ever done is like surfing. It's really harnessing the power of the waves of the earth. The ocean is mother to me." He was quiet for awhile. "Surfing is like a drug. You get hooked on it." Another pause. "It's the most important thing in my life." He looked down, his cheeks red. "It is amazing how much I've changed. It straightens things out for you. My mind is so clear. I can even put it into words. It makes me cry."

"It does make you cry." My eyes were glistening now.

"A day like today brings it out. The waves are real high and even though you get pounded, you start again even though it's freezing." Another long pause. "Everyone doesn't have it in them," he said in his matter of fact way, the way he says everything.

A few weeks later, I brought up the conversation again and said how much his thoughts on surfing meant to me.

"When? I don't remember what I said." He put his board under his strong tan arm and turned back to the surf.

AVA JEAN BRUMBAUM

Evan

I WAS AT FALLEN LEAF when I received the call from Ava that she was in labor. I closed up the cabin, drove the four hours to Berkeley, and went directly to her house. What a shambles! Ava, never a very meticulous housekeeper, had left in a hurry and dishes and laundry were all over the place. I knew that her husband, Lloyd, and a nurse-friend were helping her with her labor, and since this was her first baby, I expected that it might last a long time. I can't stand a mess, and as I seldom have my priorities straight when it comes to such things, I cleaned up and, after checking on progress at the hospital, fell exhausted into bed. About midnight the telephone rang. It was Ava wanting me to come at once. She was very excited—she had a boy! I didn't expect the hospital to let me in at that time of night, but things had changed since I had my babies. Not only did they let me in, but when I walked into the room where mother, son, and father were, a nurse handed me the little wrapped-up bundle that was Evan. I still remember the feel, the solidness, the weight. With that first touch I bonded. I have marveled at the mystical thing that happens. Was it because he was my first grandchild? Is there something in our natures that recognizes like genes?

I wasn't the only one to bond. On the occasion of his baptism when he was a year old, there were about ten adults—grandparents, parents, uncles, and aunts—who spent an entire afternoon watching and admiring whatever the little fellow did as he crawled around on the floor and we passed him from lap to lap.

Evan and I had our initial confrontation the first time I took him home with me when he was about eleven months old. He didn't want to have his diapers changed. We had a house guest at that time, a young musician named Nicky. It took Nicky and me at least twenty minutes to hold down that writhing, screaming little body so I could put the diaper pins in without stabbing him.

The next such encounter came on Christmas Day when Evan was two-and-a-half. I think it was the last one, because I was learning about strong wills and the perils of ultimatums. The family had opened their presents and decided to go to Baker Beach for some fresh air and a run. Evan and I were the last ones out of the car. He had a cold, and I told him that he could not get out until he put his jacket on. He took a position and was not going to change. While we battled it out, the others disappeared down the beach. I wanted to be with them, and so did he. The screams were earth-shattering. I lost my temper—and then lost the contest as well, of course.

We made up, and one night during a family dinner celebration, when he was three, I left the table early to go upstairs to check on Harold, Evan's grandfather, who was too ill to come down. Just as I reached the bedroom I realized that Evan had followed me. He leaned against my leg as I stood by the bed and said, "I love you, Gram." I don't know what I had done to deserve that tribute, but the bonding strengthened another notch.

When he was nearly four I began to suspect that there was something special about him. It was about the time that Halley's Comet was appearing, and we were driving across the Bay Bridge discussing it. A month or so before, I had given him a book on the subject and we had read it together. During our discussion I realized that I had forgotten most of the significant details, but Evan, clearly, had not. He remembered almost everything we had read, and to my amazement told me that it would return in seventy-six years.

When Evan was five he went to Shell Island with me for the first time. Harold had died, and I had a fantasy about Evan learning all the unusual things one needs to know on an island, like tethering boats, firing up a wood stove, filling oil lamps. I intended to train him to be my helper. He did try his best to help, and he was good company, but by the time my son Peter and two of his friends arrived for a visit, I was so tired that I retreated and let them take him on as a project. The two friends made paper hats and, using sticks as guns, they step-marched over the entire island. Then they took him home with them on the plane.

At age six he came once more. When we visited the wonderful natural history museum in Victoria he remembered where everything was from his visit of the year before. His first desire was to see the woolly mammoth again, and he took me right to it. He knew the names of most of the shore birds, and was able to correct me. ("Gram, that's a trumpeter swan, not a whistling swan. It's bigger. And besides, that's what the sign says.") He was eight when he became fascinated with the Indian exhibits in the same museum.

When we bought the ranch in Nicasio it was a joy to see Evan and his little brother Aaron there. The boys took off up the hill together and loved to sit on a big rock halfway up, talking and fantasizing about Indians or cowboys or I don't know what. They loved each other's company, and one day on a hike, when Aaron was so tired that he sat down in the middle of a trail, Evan lifted him up and put his arm around him to help him on his way. One day I discovered on their family refrigerator a snapshot of Evan on a horse. "Happiness is riding my grandmother's horse," the caption read.

I knew it must happen that as the children grew older they would become more involved in their own activities on weekends and would not find the time to come to Nicasio so often. Soccer games, birthday parties, and just commonplace activities with friends have kept them busy. Their sister, Elise, who is six, comes more often, but that, too, will change with time.

Evan is sweet with Elise. He seems to understand her need for attention and physical contact. He is patient when she hangs all over him, as she recently did while we were standing in line at a restaurant. The night their mother died he had said to me, "Poor Elise. She won't even remember." He understood immediately the consequences of what had happened, though we all worry a bit because he has never cried, never shown any emotion, or talked about his mother. Whatever his feelings are about that night, he keeps them to himself—as he does about most things.

Evan is thirteen now, the tallest boy in his class. At last he has grown up to his front teeth. He has thick, dark hair which he cares about keeping immaculately clean and brushed. There is a dark fringe appearing on his upper lip, his voice is deep, and on the telephone I have trouble telling it from his father's. He still plays soccer, but he also earns ten dollars a game refereeing for the younger boys. He is a prodigious reader: during one week while visiting us at Fallen Leaf he read six large grown-up books, two of them in the series *The Clan of the Cave Bear.* He read Tolkien's *Trilogy of the Ring* when he was nine, now reads everything he can find about King Arthur, knighthood, and castles, and science fiction as well. His father says his brain is like a sponge, soaking up, and retaining, whatever he sees or reads, and his knowledge of so many things, like ancient and natural history, astonishes me. It will be fascinating to watch as he ripens into manhood.

Aaron

"AARON, IT'S FIVE-THIRTY. Time to get up and catch our plane for Shell Island."

"Thanks, Gram, for waking me up," came the cheerful reply as he bounced out of bed. Hard to believe such good nature from an eight-year-old who hadn't gone to bed too early.

It was Aaron's turn to spend a week with us at our island in British Columbia. His brother, Evan, had been there the year before; and his sister, Elise, age five, did not feel happy about leaving her daddy, so she had not yet come. It was necessary to catch a seven o'clock Airporter bus to make our nine o'clock plane and we were forty-five minutes from Larkspur, where we would board it. It would be a long day—longer, it turned out, than we had bargained for.

Everything went according to plan until we reached Seattle, where we needed to change planes for the Victoria Airport. We were notified of a delay. Every fifteen minutes or so there would come the announcement that we would be boarding shortly. We read stories, ate ice cream cones, and after three hours Aaron remarked, the hint of a twinkle in his big, brown eyes, "I think they're trying to bored us."

About 5:00 p.m. we landed in Victoria, cleared customs, picked up a rental car and a few groceries, and headed for the marina where my son Tom was to meet us in our boat. No boat. No Tom. What to do? Harold (my second husband has the same name as my first) went to the gas dock and tried to talk some boaters into taking us to our island a short distance away. No takers. Renting boats in the area is difficult; at that marina, impossible. We were told that a new marina nearer town might rent us one. Back, then, in the car to that marina where we found that boats could not be rented after five o'clock p.m. Near tears from fatigue and frustration, I finally convinced the agent to let us have one if we had it back within the hour. Offshore from the island we managed to hail Tom, who followed us back in our boat so we could return the rental boat and retrieve our luggage. There had been a misunderstanding, and he had not expected us until after dinnertime. Throughout this ordeal Aaron, though obviously tired, made not a complaint. It was after eight before I finally put a plate of pasta in front of an exhausted little boy, who was soon in bed in the little guest cabin fifty yards from our house.

After Tom and his wife left the next morning, Aaron couldn't wait to explore the island and started out, shoelaces untied as usual. He had been there two years before and wanted to revisit his favorite spots. He had found a little place on a rocky cliff where he could curl up on a shelf to watch the water. This year, though, he was too big. On the trails in the woods he loved to run ahead of me, hiding behind a tree and jumping out to surprise me. He never tired of that. He collected black crows' feathers on the trails and once in a while a large eagle feather. He found shells and pretty stones on the beach by the score, all of which, when the time came, he of course wanted to take home

We marveled at his appetite. Harold tried to make some fudge with him one day and Aaron called the failure "chocolate sand," but even that didn't spoil it for him. The skinny little boy ate at least a dozen pancakes for breakfast, often second helpings of pasta or whatever else he liked (which was just about everything). Harold cooked him a turkey dinner one night because he had said that was his favorite meal. He enjoyed it all right, but then let it be known that it wasn't as good as the one his dad's friend Larry cooked at Thanksgiving. Harold took this candor in stride, conveyed as it was with such charm.

At that time of year in the North, the daylight lasts until nearly ten o'clock p.m. Eating dinner on the beach and then toasting that perfect marshmallow over the fire was a special treat for Aaron. Even he couldn't eat all the marshmallows he cooked.

One day he and I drew pictures, and each of us had to guess what the other had drawn. He drew a house and, hinting, he said, "It's a place where there are some people I really care about." It was his home, of course, and I wondered if he weren't just a little bit homesick. His mother had died two years before, and of her three children he had expressed his grief most openly, sobbing often and being sent home from school early by an understanding teacher on the day his classmates were making Mother's Day cards, which had been more than he could take. Still, his father had managed to create a loving home, and the four of them were wonderfully close.

In the evenings we played games. Sometimes it was dominoes, but the favorite of us all was a game he had brought with him for my birthday. It is called Rummikub, but we call it Tile Rummy, and it was interesting for grandparents and grandchild alike. Aaron came close, but he never quite finished first. He was a good sport, but we could see that he wanted to win desperately, so we decided to engineer a game one night so he could do so. Near the end of the game he looked at me plaintively and said, "Gram, would you help me?" He was so eager, and when he did win the expression of joy is a memory I cherish.

One day we put down a trap and caught a fine Dungeness crab. The crab hung on to the trap and we had trouble making it let go. Finally it was in the bottom of the boat and we had a hilarious time catching it and getting it into a bucket of sea water. Aaron helped me clean the crab on a rocky point, Harold boiled it, and Aaron ate it all for lunch. It was that day that he saw the eagles for the first time and also saw his first otter. When he went to bed that night he said, "Gram, this has been the best day of my life!"

When bedtime came on the night before he was to leave, he looked longingly at the beds in the living room. "I wish I could sleep there," he said. The little guest cabin was kind of far away and lonely, but with him in the living room Harold and I would have had to go to sleep ourselves because there wasn't enough light in the bedroom to read by. But he hadn't complained and had willingly slept alone all the other nights, so I went for his sleeping bag and he snuggled down in the cozy, warm living room as we gladly went to bed.

The next day, having been rewarded by his hasty, bashful hugs, Harold and I waved Aaron goodbye at the airport boarding gate and felt a huge emptiness. As we walked slowly toward the car he observed, "That's one child I could have around all the time, and there aren't many I could say that about."

AVA JEAN BRUMBAUM

Elise

"BIRTHING" IS OFTEN A SOCIAL occasion these days. At Alta Bates Hospital in Berkeley, the "birthing room" I saw in 1988 had a double bed along one wall and chairs set around the perimeter of the other three sides—big enough for a party. I had never attended such a party but my daughter, Ava, who was a nurse, had invited her brothers for her first two deliveries, as I found out after the event. I hadn't asked, as it seemed to me to be a family affair: perhaps Mother/Mother-in-law might not be welcome.

When the third child was soon to arrive I told Ava that I would like to be there. However, when the call came that she was on her way to the hospital, I was on the tennis court at Stinson Beach. Arriving at Alta Bates, I found Elise on her way to the nursery for her first bath. That reddish, flailing, squalling little creature didn't show much promise at less than one hour old, but fortunately, eight years later she is a slim, athletic little girl who is bright and pretty, with her mother's dark, silky hair and hazel eyes. Her name is Ava Elise, the fifth generation to bear the name Ava. Her great-great-grandmother was Ava Maria, her great-grandmother was Ava Elizabeth, her grandmother (me) is Ava Jean, and her mother was Ava Elizabeth also.

At three years of age Elise and my husband Harold had a war of wills—"No veggies, no dessert." It was a loser all around, and Gramp Harold decided not to take on that strain of obstinacy again. The strong will and knowing what she likes and doesn't like still makes life harder for Gram sometimes when it comes to which clothes for her to wear or which food to eat, or how to fix her hair.

The events of the night Elise's mother died are vividly imprinted on my memory. We were at home in Nicasio when Ava's good friend called to say she had the three children and that Ava was in the hospital with an asthma attack—"Come at once!" Harold and I didn't talk much on the way over—each of us had our own thoughts we were afraid to express. When we drove up to the emergency room and I saw my doctor-brother and his daughter standing on the ramp, I knew the worst. While he told me the news and was hugging me, I saw Ava's three children coming down the ramp with the friend who had called me earlier. I tried to hug all three at once. Evan, then ten, walked off behind the shrubbery, expressionless. Aaron, eight, was sobbing violently. Elise, then four, was completely bewildered. She wasn't crying; she didn't understand the meaning of the strange things that had happened that night which would change her life forever.

The children were taken home, while Harold and I met Ava's husband, Lloyd, in the emergency room and said our goodbyes to Ava. The ER nurses were crying, as were three of Ava's nurse-friends who, mysteriously, had heard and appeared so quickly.

When we returned to Ava's home the children were in bed and some nice person I had never seen before was reading to Elise, who was soon asleep.

Friends and neighbors helped Lloyd for weeks and even months with hot dinners delivered almost daily to the door. I wanted to help, too, especially with Elise, but it was impossible to do so for a long time. When I came to take her home with me one day she clung to her father, wrapping her arms around his leg and crying. Naturally we decided not to push her then. It was months before she would leave him, but finally she came along with me.

It has been our custom to have one of Ava's three children visit us at Shell Island each summer. When Elise was six it was her turn. Lloyd's sister, who lives in Seattle, helped her transfer to a plane for the Victoria Airport where we would meet her. For weeks we had tried to prepare her for the visit by talking about the games we would play, the wildlife, the ferry boats, before she finally agreed to come.

The first day, while exploring the beach she had a painful fall off a log, landing on her knee. The wail went up—"Daddy, Daddy, Daddy"—and Harold and I feared the visit would be a disaster. Somehow we managed to distract her and the rest of the week was a joy. We made sandwiches out of sand for a Barbie doll picnic, we had canoe rides with curious seals popping their heads up to see who we were, and the most fun for Elise was following a young ornithologist around the island and finding the song sparrow nests into which she had put plastic eggs. (Her intent was to determine who the predators were by examining the nature of the damage to the eggs. She decided it was the crows.)

Two years later, when Elise was eight, she came to Shell Island again. I became very aware that the child was emerging into an interesting girl with a distinct personality. She showed her first interest in clothes, she cared about her hair and loved to brush it, trying different styles. She had good facility with the beginner's needlepoint kit I had given her for her birthday. When we three played our favorite game called Tile Rummy each night (Harold and she had become pals long since), she amazed us with her ability to plan moves almost as well as we could. Her favorite activity was to walk around the island. One evening we found a baby seal lying very quietly on the beach. The little creature hardly moved, but past experience had taught us not to touch it. We could see "mom" out in the bay watching. Elise was excited and ran back to the house for her camera. Happily, the next morning the little thing was gone, so (or so we hoped) it had not been sick and dying after all. An otter sighting delighted her, as did the resident heron, the eagles, even the gulls and the comical crows.

One day Elise said, "Gram, which do you like better, Nicasio or

Shell Island?" "I love them both," I answered. "I feel very lucky to have two such nice places." "Oh," she said, "I love it *here*. I would like to stay here forever—except that I'd miss my family." I decided that this granddaughter was okay—not fearful of snakes or spiders, loving all living creatures, appreciating the beauty of her surroundings, and enjoying the subtleties of Winnie the Pooh as much as I did—and still do.

Two weeks ago, the Berkeley schools had two holidays (staff enrichment days, they were called), and Elise came to Nicasio. On Monday she went with me to the Nicasio school, where at the start of each week I help the kindergarten/first grade teacher. On these Mondays the children draw a picture in their journals of some special weekend activity and the teacher and I help them write a short story about it. Elise is in the third grade, so she too could help with the writing and spelling. Later she also helped me correct first grade math papers. Then, at eleven-thirty, we headed out to the Dance Palace in Point Reyes Station for my "gentle yoga" class. The teacher was helpful, and Elise followed everything we did. That afternoon we made bran muffins together. She measured correctly, stirred vigorously, and licked the spoon enthusiastically, though we both knew that dough with raw egg in it is a no-no.

On Tuesday we went to the San Francisco Zoo, where my good friend and former neighbor Hopey works in the development office. The Insect Room with its cases full of crawling things was of special interest to Elise, as was feeding the goats in the petting zoo. But Hopey had some extra-special treats in store for us as well. At two o'clock each day the big "cats" get fed in their cages arranged around a large room, and Hopey took us into the kitchen where their keeper, Jack, was cutting up huge chunks of horse meat. Then on to the feeding area, and when Jack pushed some meat into the cage of an enormous black-and-white Siberian tiger named Charlie, which pounced on it with a ferocious roar, Elise jumped back—but was soon up close to its cage again.

Next, on we went to the giraffe enclosure, where the keeper tore off acacia branches for us to hold up to those big mouths as they bent their long necks over the fence—which Elise found to be even more fun than feeding the horses in Nicasio. There was a sweet baby there, too, some twenty feet tall, or so it seemed, but too shy to approach the fence. The keeper told us that giraffes deliver standing up and the baby drops about six feet to the ground—thump. What a welcome into the world! Finally, Hopey gave Elise a little stuffed baby rhino, since we had not been able to see the real one—the newest baby at the Zoo—her mother declining to bring him out of their shelter that day.

Driving home, I asked Elise what she had liked best. She was thoughtful for a moment, then said, simply, "Hopey." How neat! I thought. She really is discerning.

What fun I am having with this little girl who reminds me so much of another little girl, my companion of many years ago.

A Far Country

JEAN-LOUISE N. THACHER

Zafrané

"IT'S TERRIBLE THE PROBLEMS we're having with the sand out there," said Mouldy, looking at us across the oilcloth-covered table in the coffee shop. Nobody said anything so I figured that my daughter Edith and her roommate Susan knew what their Tunisian friend was talking about. The girls had been teaching in Ksar Hellal for almost a year with the Peace Corps. They were enjoying the beaches, the ancient sites, and the friendly Tunisians.

"What's happening?" I inquired.

Mouldy explained his family had come from a village called Zafrané on the edge of the Sahara. They still owned a large date grove. It was time to send some supplies to the caretaker.

"I'm worried about the future. The wells are drying up and the sand is moving in. Tomorrow, I'll send my truck to Zafrané with supplies. Pollination time is coming."

Tomorrow, unfortunately, Edith had to teach school.

"How long a trip is it to Zafrané?" I inquired.

"Two hours out, two hours back, two hours there, my manager will be driving. I can't take the time." Mouldy paused and looked at me. "Would you like to go?" he said. "It's a dry, dusty trip!"

119

Edith smiled at me, "Mom, you better go."

The manager drove the ancient Ford truck filled with drinking water, cans of gasoline, tinned food, bottled soft drinks, and other supplies. Since Ali, the manager, spoke no English and my Arabic was very limited, there was little conversation.

Zafrané proved to be a tiny, clustered, dusty village like dozens of other tiny, clustered, dusty villages near oases in southern Tunisia. The last stop on an ancient, abandoned track, now barely visible, across the desert. There was a palm grove with alfalfa growing underneath, a well, olive trees, and sandy paths to mud huts with thatched roofs. Sheep, goats, donkeys, and camels occasionally entered the scene going to and from pasture. Women dressed in pink or purple wandered to the well with gourds and amphora or rusty kerosene tins on their shoulders. Village dogs, tails dragging, slunk among the huts. Three boys ran along laughing and rolling tin hoops on the path.

We drove to the palm grove. The caretaker Hikmut greeted us and offered us spicy lemon tea in glasses. Then, he showed us around the palm grove. The trunks of the trees were marked with the stubs of leaves pruned long ago. The top of each trunk bore a crown of shining leaves ten to twenty feet long. The female palms were in full bloom, many at a height of sixty to eighty feet. They were ready for hand pollination. A single bunch could weigh nearly twenty pounds and carry more than a thousand dates.

Hikmut obviously loved his trees as he patted their trunks and called them by name. He wanted to talk about the individual trees but since I couldn't follow the conversation I went for a walk.

High dunes enclosed the scene on three sides and seemed to hold the village to the earth. The dry dunes were tall and covered with patterns blown by the wind. Flaky streaks of sand had blown off the tops of the dunes and threatened to hide the village. In the distance, Zafrané looks golden and serene guarded by the huge dunes. The dome of the marabout shrine gleams and glows.

On the fourth side, the coastal road and the unpaved desert tracks meet. Salt slowly encroached on the sand. The flat spaces stretch endlessly beyond the clustered dunes. Sweeping curvy lines are drawn by the wind in the sand as the ocean does on the water near the shore. Here and there palm trees stand in the hollows of the dunes. The dunes stretch hill after hill until the very highest rises in special splendor guarding the background. The sun makes hollows and ridges stand out from the surface. The dunes seem somehow primitive, untouched, primeval pure and simple. There are no footprints, nothing to indicate humanity or break the undulating pattern. It is hard to decide whether or not to climb the dunes and destroy the unmarred simplicity. Knowing that one of the greatest deserts of the world, the Sahara, lay just beyond made the decision easy. There was no choice.

The sand was sparkling, dry and fine. Each step on the steep surface caused a tiny avalanche. The rosy glow in the sky got stronger and stronger with the sinking sun. Climbing was slow and the further above the earth the sand lay, the deeper one sank at each step. At last, the crest of the highest dune was reached. The wind had shaped it into a magnificent rounded peak. It was rosy and pink with golden underlayers and rosy tinges. There was peace and beauty everywhere. Nothing extra. Just pure sand dunes.

As the sun slipped down, a slight breeze came up and the sand began stirring and blowing lightly off the crest of the dunes. It was blowing towards Zafrané. I turned towards the village and saw, beyond the dunes, piles of sand that almost obscured some house walls and were submerging baby palms. A small boy walked across the dunes. He climbed lightly up to greet me.

"E-english? Amerikanyia? Fransawi? Sigariya-candy, money, pen," he importuned. It sounded like his complete English vocabulary.

"La!" (no) I responded sharply. He was destroying my special mood. He looked disappointed and turned to go away. I relented.

"*Aish, yissawa hunnack?*" (What happened over there?), I inquired; pointing to the mounds covered with sand.

"Just before I came, the sand took my parent's house away." He watched me closely as he spoke.

"What could you do?"

"We went away to there." He pointed to Zafrané.

Shadows were beginning to reach the village. Some of the huts were already covered with darkness. The glazed dome of the marabout shrine still shone in the light. I felt apprehensive. Now the wind was blowing the sand towards the village. The shadows were growing.

"What are you going to do?"

"Go home and eat," he said with practical assurance. "The sun has set."

"No, I mean about the sand."

"About the sand? When it comes we go."

"But—but what about all the date palms? They have been growing a long time. They must give many dates."

"Date palms die too. Choke like a man!"

The young face seemed old now. He had seen a great deal. He had much to remember.

"How will you live then?" I knew all the things the date palm provided, food, shelter, timber, fibre, paper starch, wax, wine, tannin and thatching materials. It was an essential plant in the desert.

"Allah will provide." He answered earnestly.

It was impossible to pursue this line of questioning in the face of such earnest faith.

"Do you like the sand?" I was truly interested and added defensively, "It's good for running, for rolling, for jumping!"

With that the little boy turned and began to roll down the steep dune, sending up great waves and sprays of sand as he rolled over and over laughing and smiling at me. I continued to watch him as he struggled up the bare slope again, his bare feet starting little avalanches of sand as he came up the dune.

"But the sand is hot in summer. Hot to walk on—nothing can grow—," I began again.

"It moves, always it moves—it can go anywhere." He said almost proudly. "Perhaps some day it will cover the earth. My sand!" He smiled proudly.

What could I say? How could I make him think about the threat to his family, his village, his very existence by this steadily shifting menace?

"It's very strong. How can you fight it?"

"Fight it? Who says fight the sand?"

"Down the road they have put the palm fronds in the sand to keep it back. They are woven very tightly."

"Soon the sand comes and covers them."

"Yes, but it holds it for a while."

"What's the use only for a while?"

"More years for the trees to grow, to raise the dates to live here."

"Always it comes."

The sun had long gone. It was getting quite dark. The glow had left the sky.

"But the trees, they will be covered to their heads. They will be smothered. They will die."

"Too bad, they are not my trees."

"Surely the government, surely someone can do something."

"Yes, yes the big trucks come. They take the sand. They take it away."

"Away? Away where? What do they do with it?"

"They dump it out there!" He pointed to the Grand Erg behind us.

"Out there? But it will come back!"

"It comes back and they take it again and again until there is too much!"

I looked down at my small friend. I saw the cynicism, the pessimism about his fate, and yet a strong pride in the power of the sand. Then we both heard the eerie sound, that few ever hear. The sand was singing. The wind, the dampness, the heat, all have to be just right.

"Listen, the sand calls to the *mahout*. It is a warning."

The little boy pointed to the old, cracked marabout shrine on a low hill just beyond the village. When would the sand siege begin? He looked apprehensive. He asked me to come back to the village with him. We walked to his hut. A mangy yellow dog gave a few hoarse barks. His vocal chords had been cut. Voices came out of the black hole of the shack.

"*Ma, salama.* (Good-bye), *Allah ya kefik.*" (God be with you). He said staring at me as he turned to enter his hut.

"*Fi mani la.*" (And also with you) I responded close to tears. Then I heard his family as they welcomed him.

"*La bes*" (Greetings), "*Ala aiynek*" (Welcome), "*Shawalid*" (How are you?).

I headed towards the small space where a few men played a sort of domino game. There were several spectators. One of the green wooden tables was empty.

"*Chai, min fudluk*" (Tea, please). The waiter poured the hot tea, fragrant with lemon and sugar, into a small glass in a metal frame with a handle.

"*Talaatash, millimes*" (Thirteen millimes)" My brass coins clinked on the copper tray.

"About this sand—" I began. The waiter seemed not to understand my Arabic and turned his back. What about the sand? Must it cover the earth? Must the palms smother in it? Must the village disappear? Must the people move on forever to stay a few years ahead of the sand, until they get too tired and are covered by it? Now I have a feeling of slowly encroaching tragedy and oblivion. Nowhere in Tunisia could I find the answer, not on the ride back, not from Mouldy or Edith or her friends. The problem haunted me.

Three years later, after Edith had left Tunisia and Susan and Mouldy were living in Brooklyn with their twin boys, I returned to Tunisia and hired a guide in Tunis who came from Zafrané. He failed to find his village. At one place, the dunes looked familiar but then how could they? They are constantly shifting. In the distance something caught the sun's rays. It gleamed brilliantly in the desert. It must be the gold on the roof of the marabout shrine.

MARY THACHER

My Indian Encounter

I OPENED MY EYES and watched a warm pink glow gradually suffuse the early morning sky.

"Where am I?" I felt the heat of the day permeating my room. Slowly it dawned upon me that I was at the Taj Hotel in Bombay.

"How did I get here?"

It was December fifth. Less than ten days ago Carter and I had given Thanksgiving dinner at our home in San Francisco. It was about eight in the evening and the last of some thirty family members and friends had left. I had just about finished putting away those numerous "possessions" which rarely make their appearance outside of their cupboards.

The telephone rang. There was a cable for me: "Meet me in Bombay. Do not chicken out." Signed Polly. If it had not been for the "do not chicken out" I would have ignored it. One and only daughter Polly had been attending Grinnell College in Grinnell, Iowa, and was now spending her junior year at University of Poona, about four hours from Bombay. Polly had been the easiest child imaginable so it was a shock to find that in her junior year in college, I was encountering a new individual. In her quiet way, she obviously disapproved of me. Not so her father. All of which made my ego plummet. So I was not going to take that cable seriously without more information. I spent several long nights trying to reach Polly by phone in a place thirteen hours ahead of us. I finally heard a clear little voice saying "Yes, I truly want you to come." I was fully aware that Polly did not want me solely for my charming company. She needed my wallet and also wanted to have someone with whom to travel and visit the art centers she longed to see.

I decided to go. Polly never received the cable telling her the date and time of my arrival.

On the day of departure, my husband sent another cable reiterating the arrival time, which Polly did receive on the very day she was to set off on a short trip with some fellow students.

I will never forget the relief I felt as I descended the steps of the plane into a sea of pushing and shoving Indians in the Bombay airport and finally spotted my dear, short Polly with the long pigtail down to her waist.

I had made reservations at the Taj Hotel, a real landmark in Bombay, situated right on the waterfront and built in the grand British style of the last century. The receptionist apologized because the only rooms available were in the old wing, and with very high ceilings and a large old-fashioned bathroom. Polly shrieked with delight when she saw the deep marble bathtub. She had not had a bath since arriving in India. Polly had been fortunate in living with a truly lovely family, which consisted of Mr. and Mrs. Rada and their two girls, Para and Serena, aged fifteen and twelve. Mr. Rada was the head of the chemistry department at the university. The Rada family lived in a simple, fairly new, apartment building, containing probably twenty units. The apartment consisted of a living room and eating area combined, and two bedrooms. The rooms were small but cheerful. Once a week you could fill a pail of water in the bathroom and put into it an electric gadget that would heat the water and then you could wash yourself. The rest of the time, cold water was used for everything, including the washing of dishes. So you can imagine Polly's delight upon seeing that gorgeous bathtub. She filled it as high as possible and with water as hot as possible, and in an instant she was immersed. "This is the greatest!" I was barely able to pry her away for dinner.

The next day we went to an Indian travel agent recommended to us by the hotel. The office was reminiscent of an Indian movie, complete with rickety elevator which took us to an upper floor. Tea was served immediately by a turbaned servant with much bowing, and a very unctuous travel agent appeared. We told him the places we wished to visit and immediately, and with great enthusiasm, he sketched out elaborate plans, including cars to meet us at airports and railway stations. I did not know India, but I felt I was being ensnared. I looked at Polly and could see that she had the same mistrust. It was obvious that he thought we were some rich Americans. With great difficulty, we managed to extricate ourselves.

We decided to try American Express. By great good fortune, a very charming and cultured woman took care of us. She seemed genuinely impressed with the fact that Polly had been studying in India for a year and also knew the local Marathi dialect. She worked out a superb three-week trip for us which included both simple hotels and the most famous ones. And no cars to meet us.

We began our trip to southern India. We stayed in a resort hotel on the coast. Unfortunately, it was a week before the tourist season began and besides one elderly gentleman, we were the only ones there. It was quite dismal. We took a walk along the deserted beach and suddenly we saw a dead body lying in the sand, face up. We had almost stepped upon it. I can still see his brown wrinkled skin with the foam on his beard. When we returned to the hotel and reported the event, no one was interested. "By tomorrow he will be washed up to the next beach." We were totally shaken by the experience.

We resumed our walk along the lovely beach but in the opposite direction. A moment later, the most enchanting Indian child approached us with a wide-open smile. His straight white teeth sparkled in his dusky brown face. In one hand he was clasping a little boy of about three. In the other, he was holding a bag of shells for sale. He proudly displayed them on the sand. He was irresistible and we bought several pure white conches from him. One turned out to still have a live snail in it, which proved to be a smelly disaster in my suitcase.

When evening came, I said, "Polly, let's go down to the bar for a cocktail before dinner." Polly replied, with criticism in her voice, "I certainly don't want anything to drink. In fact, I'm not hungry and I would rather stay up here and read." I was very taken aback and disappointed. I went downstairs and ate by myself while reading the guidebook. When I returned, Polly was reading in bed, propped up by many pillows. She said very little. I can remember getting out my journal and trying to console myself by describing how gloomy and let down I felt.

By the next morning I had made a resolve. Polly was full of cheerfulness as we dressed for breakfast. Just before leaving the room I said, "Polly, I want to talk to you. I have come halfway around the world to be with you because you asked me. But I do not intend to travel with you if you are going to be critical of me. And I do not intend to eat meals alone. And I do intend to have a drink in the evening if I wish. If this is a problem for you, I have no qualms about packing up and leaving for home tomorrow. It's December and there are many enjoyable events going on in San Francisco." Polly said nothing.

That evening, without being asked, Polly accompanied me to the bar and had some fruit juice. By the end of the trip, she even began to have some rum in her juice. It was as though a miracle had occurred. There was a hundred-percent change in her attitude. From that day on, Polly was the most delightful and perceptive companion and we never exchanged a cross word with each other.

From there we flew to New Delhi where we stayed at the Oberoi Hotel. It is justly famous and elegant. Our room was not. We were above the kitchen on the second floor. All day long and well into the night the smell of rancid fat and spices wafted through the vents in our room.

One evening Polly decided to go and see an Indian movie and eat at the coffee shop when she returned. I thought I might as well go to the lobby and watch the passing parade. I now understand so well why those forlorn old ladies were always sitting in plush chairs in the lobbies of fine hotels. It was an auspicious time for weddings and good Hindus only married in that period. As a result, many wedding receptions were going on at the Oberoi. Such handsome men and beautiful women passed by dressed in magnificent saris and wearing opulent jewelry. Never have I seen such a striking group of people with their warm brown skin, shiny black hair, and colorful attire.

I decided to go to the Oberoi Grill for dinner, by this time feeling rather forlorn myself and also very hungry. An Indian, probably in his late forties, as elegantly dressed as a native Londoner in his dark blue pinstriped suit and blue shirt, approached me as I was waiting to ask the maitre d' for a table. He very politely introduced himself, "Would you care to join me for dinner? We can each pay our own bill but I could guide your choices to the most savory dishes while telling you about Delhi, my native city. And I am feeling very lonely because my wife recently passed away."

Eating alone at restaurants is one of my least favorite occupations, so after a moment, I decided to say "Yes." We were given a nicely situated table. He had a cocktail and I had the wine he recommended. He suggested a grilled red snapper topped with a mixture of coriander, red chilies, and chopped tomatoes. Both its aroma and taste were superb. His descriptions of India were lively and interesting. "I work at the Indian Embassy and as a result, I meet many foreigners. But for the past year, I have been so overcome with grief over the loss of my wife that I have been almost a recluse. And I have wanted to be with my two young daughters as much as possible. But now I am trying to resume a more normal life." My heart did go out to him.

Towards the end of dinner, he said, "Do come with me to the Skylight Room, as my guest. They have a lovely view of Delhi and wonderful music for dancing. I know you would enjoy it." In spite of the fact that I love to dance, I knew that was not to my taste. He kept urging me and I kept reiterating my refusal. He excused himself for a moment. The moment extended on and on. Finally light dawned on me and I knew I had been taken. The waiters all looked in other directions as I asked for the bill and paid for both dinners. I definitely had the impression that this was a regular occurrence and so with as much dignity as I could muster, I left the restaurant.

During the next few days, I kept a watchful eye for my elegant Indian. Suddenly I saw him at the same moment he spotted me. He quickly walked in another direction. I pursued him and he had to stop. "You did your American acquaintance an injustice. You brightened my evening. If you had admitted that you did not intend to pay for dinner, I still would have considered the evening worth it. But this way, you left me humiliated." I turned and walked away. I had an Indian encounter and I had become a little wiser.

BETTY WHITRIDGE

Taxi! Taxi!

CARLESS FRED AND BETTY are glad that a motley array of cabs and drivers sits perpetually in front of our Nairobi Safari Club home. We are commanded by the International Executive Service Corps, the volunteer agency which sends retired American executives to advise foreign business: "Only ride in 'Kenyacab,' the government-owned line. Clean, reliable cars, licensed drivers." Daily, we search but no such vehicle ever appears. We choose instead one of the high, black London cabs.

The rules again: "Always agree on price before boarding. Nairobi cabs have no meters." Ever obedient, Fred and Betty demand: "How much to the Norfolk Hotel?"

"Five hundred Kenya shillings," the driver replies.

"But that's fifteen dollars, and the Norfolk is only three blocks," says indignant, city-wise Fred. He is a great walker, longtime climber of San Francisco hills. His greatest sorrow is being forbidden to walk in the dangerous streets of Nairobi.

Pontifically important in brass-buttoned, heavily epauletted, gold-braided, red Admiral's uniform, the Club's fat, ever-unhelpful doorman approaches. He recognizes resident unpaid volunteers as not big tippers. Smiling oilily, he assures us that this is a *very* fair price. "Maybe so, but we're not going to pay it," Fred vows. "Okay, I'll take you for 250 Kenya shillings," the wooing driver cheerfully concedes. Better to have tried and lost than never to have tried at all! Two hundred fifty Kenya shillings is still $7.50 for a three-block ride, but in we hop, flushed with our victory of sorts.

Surprise! It looked like a London cab, but is a shabby derelict— high ceilinged and roomy, yes, but with spring-sprung seats, ragged, filthy upholstery, cracked paint, non-functioning windows. Definitely a belle past her prime. Later we learn that old London cabs are sent to Nairobi to die. The entire fraternity of Safari Club cab-stand drivers smilingly gathers, heroically pushing our high, regal black vehicle to get it started. This, we find, is the usual ignition mode of most Kenya cars. Off we roll on our $7.50, three-block, springless, moldy, dusty ride.

In the Norfolk's pleasant, busy sidewalk cafe, the Lord Delemere, we indulge in the traditional amusement of people watching. From its menu we order what is listed as "hot snacky and nice" with icy "Tuskers," the delicious Kenya beer. After eating, we approach the Norfolk's taxi stand. Many "Kenyacabs" stand here. (South of the equator, the *last* cab goes first, water drains from the tub in an opposite direction, different stars in the sky.) The Norfolk's less fancily costumed doorman is on *our* side. He tells the driver of the clean cab firmly: "That will be one hundred Kenya shillings to the Safari Club." During our months in Nairobi, the equation remains the same: one hundred Kenya shillings from Norfolk Hotel to Safari Club; 250 KSH from Safari Club to Norfolk...a firm Euclidean theorem which we are unable to understand or to alter.

On Sunday, we're off to the races. A bloodshot-eyed, scruffy cab-bie finally steps forward volunteering to take us, wait during the races, bring us back all for twenty dollars. The race track is *miles* into the country. We will obviously win many Kenya shillings on the ponies, so it's a done deal.

Stephen appears at the chosen hour in a rusty cab, fenders bent, headlights missing. There are no handles on the cab's doors, but

Stephen produces a tool and somehow opens them; we climb over the crumbling running boards. Stephen slams the wobbly door and closes it again with the tool. We are aboard.

Cautionary words again from Mother Executive Service Corps: "Once in the cab, be sure to fasten your seat belts. Kenya traffic is highly dangerous." Good instructions except that in all our time in Kenya, we never encountered a cab with seat belts.

The Rules again: "Always lock cab door and close all the windows." Stephen's cab totally lacks locks, and the two windows that exist are immovable. The upholstery exudes stuffing in fluffy tufts, the floor's carpet is gone, steel bones exposed. Where ere I move, twitch, or squirm, I'm still sitting impaled on protruding springs. But forget the springs. Fred has somehow sprung us from our Sunday Dead Hotel Prison.

Ever optimistic, Fred beams: "Isn't this great! We're out of that dead hotel with the loud street music and off to the races."

But will we ever get there? The engine of Stephen's cab emits most ominous coughs, black smoke, sighs, and groans.

Finally we chug and lurch into the manicured grounds of the famous Kenya Jockey Club. Sputtering down the avenue of blooming jacaranda trees, Stephen parks amongst the Mercedes, Land Rovers, Jaguars, and club-emblazoned Bentleys.

"I'll be right here—will you be able to identify me?" Stephen solicitously asks. We think that we will.

On another evening, our journey to a dinner party at Alan Bobbe's Bistro requires, of course, a taxi. Perhaps I am a bit more excited than Fred by our plunge into Nairobi's Society. Fabled Alan Bobbe's is Nairobi's Postrio, Masas, Stars, Le Cirque, with a long colorful history. Site of Beryl Markham's rendezvous, Ernest Hemingway's not always moveable feasts, Isak Dinesen's tête-à-tête with Denys Finch-Hatton. This has called for a 500 Kenya shilling hairdo and the "one silk dress" prescribed by the Executive Service Corps.

Bobbe's Bistro is only two long blocks from the Safari Club. These two long blocks, however, are in the heart of downtown Nairobi and lined with sinister-looking, crowded, noisy bars, knots of lolling, idle men amongst dilapidated buildings, piles of rubble, dark vacant lots heaped with rat-infested garbage. Even without the Instructions, we wouldn't *want* to walk any more than we'd like to walk through San Francisco's Tenderloin District.

So! Voila! Here we are at the Taxi Stand again, hoping that Stephen will be off duty. But lo! A London taxi door opens and out from the crowd of gossiping, card-playing cabbies steps our charioteer Stephen. We are invisible to all other cabbies—we are Stephen's and his alone.

"Jambo! Mamma! Daddy! You go to Carnivore maybe?" The wretched doorman and the ranks of cabbies are forever touting Carnivore. It is a restaurant which serves ostrich, lizard, zebra, elephant, giraffe, gnu, warthog steaks, and has a red-hot girlie show. Tourists flock there.

"No, not Carnivore, just Alan Bobbe's—how much?" None of the cabbies or the imperious doorman has ever heard of this legendary watering spot. There are no street numbers in all of Nairobi—destinations are found by the names of buildings. This unique system usually works all right in downtown Nairobi with big, well-known buildings. In the suburbs and outlying villages mystery and chance prevail.

"Alan Bobbe's is in the Esso Petroleum Building," we tell them.

"Oh yaas! Esso Building." The cabbies and doorman are all smiles. "That will be 500 Kenya shillings."

"Oh no," Fred and I shout in unison. *We* know where it is too—just two blocks down Koinage Street where we are standing.

"Okay, 100 Kenya shillings," they cheerfully concede.

Stephen flings wide the creaking rusty door of our cab. We hope that our elegant hosts won't witness our Cinderella-ish arrival in this incredible coach.

Ragged, bleary-eyed Stephen in his tattered cap guides old Rusty chugging and puffing through madly roaring traffic into the complicated roundabout. We are now facing the proper direction for the two-block journey.

Halfway down the first block an ear-shattering metallic screech and bang. Major cataclysmic lurching throws us on top of each other on the carpetless floor. Has a car bomb exploded? Have we been hit by a train? Have the earthquakes followed us from California? No, it's nothing really—just one of Old Rusty's wheels has fallen off and we have skidded several yards into the middle of the street.

"It's okay, Mamma, Dad," Stephen croons. "Just sit right there and I'll get you another cab." He disappears into the night. Sit we do in a springless, listing unlockable cab in this dark unsavory neighborhood.

My fears subside when Stephen returns with another driver, another cab. Fred pays Stephen the agreed-upon fee plus a little more to help repair his rusty livelihood. We transfer to the rescue vehicle, ride the one remaining block without event, pay *him*. Some kind of a record must have been set: a two-taxi ride for a two-block trip. We enter the soigné Bistro, patting our hair and straightening our disheveled clothes. Our chic hosts obviously think we're emerging from a passionate entanglement. Let 'em think so—we'll be more interesting to these naughty Brits!

JEAN-LOUISE N. THACHER

Visitors

THE SUN WAS SINKING in the dusty sky over the Red Sea. I stared at it long and hard, trying to forget Vice-President Spiro T. Agnew's aggravating visit. I hoped his plane was far over the trackless Rub-al-Khali so Arabs from neighboring Oman would have to worry about him in the summer heat should there be an accident.

This evening the sun failed to color the surrounding beige sky before appearing to squash into an oval as it dropped beyond the edge of the horizon. After the sun disappeared, a brilliant green flash lit up the sky for an instant in a remarkable combination of sky, sun, and sea.

Near the horizon where the flash had been, there were traces of the vivid color in the water. There were no waves on the Red Sea and no wind. The air was still and warm. I brushed my hand on the water in the fountain. It was almost hot.

The fountain was octagonal in design. Its edge was broad, at chair height and covered with small blue ceramic tile. In the center of the fountain was a pillar in the form of a four-pointed star. There were bird-shaped spouts through which water poured into the basin, making cooling splashy sounds. The height of the birds and the depth of the water had been carefully calculated to give the maximum sound. There were lights in the base of the fountain that made the water shine at night. I was proud of having designed the fountain in spite of a total ignorance of architectural design, meters, centimeters, and recirculating pumps. The only things I knew were what I wanted it to look like, and that the water had to make a splashing noise.

The fountain had been inspired by the first thing I had read about Saudi Arabia in a book by T.E. Lawrence: "For the Arabs, the sweetest sound in all of Arabia is the sound of falling water." As I trailed my hand in the water, I idly wondered when the birds from Europe would pause in their annual migration across Arabia to Africa to drink at the fountain. It was about time. I particularly longed to see the colorful hoopoe.

I was very tired. My anger made me tired as much as the events themselves. Being the wife of the American Ambassador has its ups and downs. The Vice-President of the United States, Spiro T. Agnew, had just completed an absolutely exhausting four-day visit from July 8 to July 11, 1971. If I had been able to admire or respect him perhaps I wouldn't have been so exhausted. As it was, I was appalled that anyone of his ilk was just a heartbeat away from running my beloved country.

The preparations for the visit had been endless. A top-secret telegram arrived informing my husband, the Ambassador, that under no circumstances was the Vice-President to receive any news either of the U.S. or elsewhere. There was no explanation. The order was a surprise, but not a real challenge. The daily newspapers and the TV were all in Arabic, the only threat was a shortwave radio, but the Secret Service could take care of that. Keeping the Vice-President ignorant of current events was not impossible.

An armored Cadillac limousine was flown out from Washington for Agnew's use. It was so low to the ground that all the speed bumps in the American Embassy compound had to be removed. Since we had to entertain him, the Secret Service crawled over the entire residence, opening drawers in our private quarters, checking closets for concealed weapons, pouring through my special gardening tools.

Our sixteen-year-old son Adam was much upset when he found one of the agents going through his tool box. Adam went up to the agent to object and heard Beatle music coming out of the agent's chest! Adam was too startled to say anything! He had never heard anyone wired for sound. (All the agents carried walkie-talkies tuned to a secret channel. When there were no messages they played music.) The American Ambassador, of course, had to entertain for the visitor. This involved giving a formal men's lunch, really a state lunch which included the Crown Prince, the Foreign Minister, assorted cabinet ministers, and senior diplomats, with a uniformed servant behind each chair along with the translators. It got off on the wrong foot because the Secret Service, contrary to Saudi custom, refused to let the Vice-President welcome Crown Prince Khalid as he descended from his limousine at the residence. The American Ambassador had to very apologetically perform the honor.

Since liquor is not allowed in the kingdom, the before-lunch drinks of fruit juice and lemon squash did not take long. The first course was homemade tomato soup. The second course was to have been baked barracuda. The Yemeni cook, Tewfik, thought it would be much more elegant to serve the rare canned crab he had located in the bazaar. The Crown Prince told the Ambassador how delicious the fish was. The Ambassador smiled and remarked that the cook had great skill with barracuda. Then, the Vice-President, a former governor of Maryland, interrupted, "This here isn't barracuda. I know Maryland crab however it's fixed."

In the awkward silence that followed, Otis, my beloved miniature champagne poodle, a gift from the Queen I'ffat, bounced into the dining room. The dining room table was long; the Vice-President was far from the door so he couldn't see what was happening. All Agnew saw was Bill Stoltzfus, the Deputy Chief of Mission at the American Embassy, rushing from his chair and, assuming that his life was in grave danger, Agnew grabbed his necktie with his left hand and appeared about to hide under the table. There was an embarrassed groan. Bill Stoltzfus swept Otis up and hurried out. Most Saudis dislike all dogs except salukis. The Vice-President slowly regained his seat and composure. The detailed way in which my children questioned me about Otis' behavior during lunch aroused certain suspicions in my mind which I didn't have time to pursue.

The rest of the lunch progressed smoothly. The Saudis were truly awed by individual apricot souffles.

The following morning at eleven o'clock the American community, some three hundred strong, gathered in our garden to hear a talk by the Vice-President. My husband introduced him in a few words. Then Spiro T. Agnew stood in front of the door to our house in his striped tie and striped seersucker suit and striped shirt, his face getting redder by the minute in the bright sunlight.

His comments were not memorable about his delight in visiting the famous desert kingdom, Arab hospitality, and how all America is grateful to all Americans working overseas. He walked into the crowd moving around, asking who was from Maryland and shaking hands, but he answered no questions.

When the American community left, the Vice-President asked for a Coca-Cola. My children and I sat with him under the thorn trees in the garden. My nineteen-year-old daughter inquired about Julie Nixon's marriage to David Eisenhower. This the Vice-President refused to describe because he said it was private. He wasn't permitted to talk about it. Scott inquired where he was going after Arabia. He was told quite briskly: "Back to Washington." Scott looked shocked, all this way for four days!

Agnew then announced that he wished to play tennis and that he wished to have the tall, athletic Bill Stoltzfus as his doubles partner. My husband decided that it would be most exciting for our sixteen-year-old son and for Bill's fifteen-year-old son to play tennis against the Vice-President. The boys were accurate with their backhand shots, placing them just out of Agnew's reach. They saw to it that the Vice-President was constantly on the run. Agnew became hot and annoyed when the boys were beating him five games to three. He ended the match by announcing he had to go swimming with

Mabel, his voluptuous secretary. The boys were furious. They were planning to tell the world they had beaten the Vice-President of the United States at tennis.

In order to keep the entourage out of the bazaar and hopefully out of trouble, some of the bazaar merchants had been persuaded to bring goods for a mini-bazaar in the Embassy. Mabel enjoyed the shops. It was my duty to tell her when the Vice-President was ready to leave. Mabel was bargaining vigorously for a pair of gold earrings. I told her the Vice-President was ready to go. She turned and looked at me, her eyes flashing: "Tell the bastard he can wait!" I stared at her, my thoughts whirling. "That's one message you must deliver yourself. The Vice-President is waiting in the car." Having made my statement, I fled.

When I arrived home I found Tewfik in an unusual fury. "That person. He has stolen one of the Ambassador's towels!" (The government-supplied linen was fit for a clinic but not for a residence, so I invested in special towels and sheets for the guest rooms and baths.) The help was well aware of the value of the velvet-textured monogrammed towels. I wondered if the fact that the towels were monogrammed with Agnew's middle initial T was the reason for the burglary. Agnew's farewell gift of a silver card tray decorated with the great seal of the United States didn't do anything to improve my impression of him. It wasn't sterling.

On July 15 it was announced that Kissinger had flown to China and talked to Zhou en Lai. Nixon was then invited to China. He accepted and hoped to attain a normalization of relations. It wasn't long before we learned how anxious Agnew had been to play the Kissinger role. He was the only person who thought he could do it. In order to keep him from making a fuss and away from the latest news, he had been sent to Saudi Arabia. President Nixon finally went to China and opened diplomatic relations on February 21, 1972. So the strange story ended.

A year and a half later, in October 1973, no one was surprised when Agnew resigned as Vice-President. He ended up in Federal Court in Baltimore pleading no contest to charges of income tax evasion on alleged bribes he received while Governor of Maryland. He was fined ten thousand dollars and put on three years' probation. Naturally, my children followed his career with grim interest. It was impossible to explain to them how Agnew became Vice-President of the United States!

With Agnew's visit over at last, I looked around my garden with delight. A gardenia was beginning to bloom in the border. I had grafted it to a sturdy Sudanese rose, hoping for more blooms. I looked at the frankincense tree sending out new shoots in the pot by the door. The mother tree grew along the spice route from Yemen that the three wise men had used. It struggled in the desert near the turnoff to Mecca. I had stolen the cutting. Some things, at least, were working.

Just then my husband appeared, walking between the topiaried pink oleander that bordered the garden. His coat was off and he carried a briefcase.

"Beenie! Guess what?" He came over and kissed me. Before I could reply he told me that we were about to have another famous visitor.

"Oh no!" I moaned. "There go the rest of the bath towels!"

"Beenie, for heaven's sake. Wait till you hear who it is!"

"Okay, somebody fun like Bob Hope or Philip Glass or Eudora Welty, Frank Sinatra or Vincent Sheean."

"No-no-no, Senator Fulbright."

"Senator Fulbright? What's he doing out here? They don't allow any of his scholars to come to Saudi Arabia. Why send him out in all this heat?" I paused and thought for a moment. "He *is* one of the wiser members of the Senate, though."

Again there were the usual preparations of cleaning and tidying, but it was a relief that the Senator did not travel with guards nor did he expect star treatment while he stayed with us. I looked up Arkansas in our encyclopedia and found that the only active diamond mine in the U.S.A. is in Murfreesboro. Helen Gurley Brown, Johnny Cash, Alan Ladd, General Douglas McArthur, Dick Powell, and Edward Durrell Stone were all born there and there were no state forests and twelve thousand Indians. Here were some non-controversial items to talk about at breakfast.

My husband told me that the State Department was delighted Senator Fulbright was coming out to Saudi Arabia. No only was he one of America's most-respected officials, but he had demonstrated interest in the Arab cause. He was working hard on an Egyptian-Israeli peace accord for which he was anxious for Saudi support.

In his book *The Price of Empire*, he wrote: "The United States had done as much for Israel as one nation can do for another—we and we alone have made it possible for Israel to exist as a state. Surely it is not too much to ask in return that Israel give up East Jerusalem and the West Bank and Gaza and acknowledge a Palestinian right to self-determination as the necessary means of breaking a chain of events that threatens everyone with ultimate ruin."

When I finished reading, I sat on the fountain waiting for my husband and Senator Fulbright to return from the airport and wondered what to say to this courageous man. I tried to remember other things I had heard about him. He had established the Fulbright Scholarships in 1946 and by now there had been 250,000 scholars including Katherine Dunham, Aaron Copland, Derek Bok, Maya Angelou, Wallace Stegner, and Butros Butros Ghalli. He had introduced legislation to pave the way for the United Nations. He had criticized Senator McCarthy's career.

That whole McCarthy episode had been acutely painful for me. As a Foreign Service wife I had to respect the views of my government and not publicly condemn McCarthy. I failed completely to understand why President Eisenhower permitted the hearings to continue when nothing had been proved and so many careers had been destroyed. I was later to be equally pained with Watergate. I felt Mrs. Nixon should divorce the President for his shifty, un-presidential behavior. Being a loyal American representative wasn't always easy. I was eager to meet Senator Fulbright, an outspoken critic of government policy. He opposed the Vietnam War, called for our withdrawal from Korea, and was Chairman of the Senate Foreign Relations Committee for sixteen years. He was a brilliant, admirable, eloquent man. What could I say to him?

Suddenly the official Chevrolet with flags flying on each bumper drew up in front of the residence. Mustafa, the chauffeur, ran around to open the door and out stepped Senator J. William Fulbright. He was a tall, thoughtful-looking man with a friendly grin. I led the way into the residence, my husband followed. Soon we were sitting in the living room drinking tea.

When I asked Senator Fulbright about his book *Arrogance of Power*, he changed the subject to Saudi customs and people, and how I liked living in Arabia. He was perfectly charming and delightful and direct. He didn't want any dinners given for him nor did he wish to attend any. He wanted to meet with officials in their offices to discuss common problems.

The following day we took the Senator for a cruise on the Embassy boat, a tired old fishing boat named the *William A. Eddy* for the first U.S. diplomatic representative to live in Saudi Arabia. It was great for fishing and for going snorkeling along the Red Sea coast and out to the small islands. There were sharks, of course, in the Red Sea, but the tropical fish were so abundant and attractive that the tiger shark rarely attacked swimmers.

Senator Fulbright, my husband, and I were snorkeling near the side of the boats when one of the marine guards accompanying us shouted loudly, "Shark! Shark! Return to the boat! I see a shark!" We quickly herded the Senator aboard and climbed on ourselves. The Senator inquired if my husband or I had seen the shark. Nik said no and I remarked that there were several lined up at the edge of the coral reef waiting politely to ask for Fulbright scholarships. Both men stared at me, then the Senator roared with laughter and my husband continued to look uneasy.

The Senator and I began devising headlines for the international press. "Saudi shark rewrites American foreign policy." "Saudi shark sharply debates Senator and Ambassador." "Saudi shark swallows U.S. foreign policy, Senator and all." "Fulbright spars with Saudi shark." "Saudi shark gets the best of Senator." By this time the Senator was gazing at me with wry skepticism when I came up with a final headline "American Senator retreats before Saudi shark in Red Sea standoff." It was a memorable afternoon.

I cannot remember the conversations at breakfast with Senator Fulbright other than that they were lively and fun. He repeated his famous statement when my husband asked him about statesmanship: "To be a statesman you must first get elected and you must not rely on government statements." He explained his votes against the Civil Rights Act of 1964 and the Voting Rights Act of 1965 as being quite necessary for him to be elected and to play a role in government policy. He did say that his great dissents were expressions of disdain for the irrational. For this reason, he voted against Senator McCarthy, he questioned the dogmas of the Cold War, he eviscerated Johnson's Vietnam War policy.

He told us his worst mistake in public life was supporting the Gulf of Tonkin resolution and the thing he was proudest of was writing the bill establishing the Kennedy Center.

He asked if it would be possible to go sightseeing. I was delighted and began my tour by telling him that Jidda meant grandmother and was named for Eve. He was delighted with the Tomb of Eve and the tale of the site of the Garden of Eden being in Mecca, thirty miles away. Eve's tomb was in a large area in the middle of town enclosed by a brick wall. It was possible to peer over the wall and see the markers of the tomb itself, which outlined an approximately eight-foot woman. Women often went to the tomb of Eve to pray to have a child.

Senator Fulbright quickly became fascinated with the old city and the houses built of coral block cut from the Red Sea reefs. There were few trees in Jidda. Coral block was the only building material. Wood from wrecked sailing ships was used for trim, shutters, doors, and balconies. The doors all had panels cut in them so that if the visitor was unknown to the host, he would have to enter the house bent over. If he was an enemy, it was easy to cut off his head when he was in this helpless position.

Coral block made a wonderful form of cooling possible. Sea water was poured inside the porous walls. It quickly evaporated in the hot sun, cooling the interior of the building. The roofs were flat for sleeping and drying laundry.

The larger of the coral block houses had a well in the basement, but most of them had to rely on the water carrier, with his great kerosene tins carried on a large yoke over his shoulders with the water splashing out as he trotted along the sandy lanes. Just before sunset the slender bedu ran around the old city with lighted lanterns swinging from the yoke across their shoulders. The lighted lanterns were delivered to various spots in the old city. The bedu put the lanterns down and untied the ropes on the lamp posts. They had to hook the lighted lanterns onto the ropes and pull them to the top of the post and twist the rope around the hook at the base. The whole sight was wonderfully timeless, magical and medieval. Senator Fulbright was delighted.

He loved wandering in the bazaar also, seeing the sights, asking me to bargain in Arabic. He did have a busy schedule of calls and appointments in Jidda, but he was always on time and impressed everyone with his charm and knowledge and interest. On his last morning, he announced he was going to Egypt and he would like to stop in Jidda before returning to Washington. We thought that was wonderful!

I inquired if there was anything to do for him while he was away. He told me he would love to have a Saudi outfit to take home. He appeared to be about the same size as Tewfik. Tewfik made the appropriate purchases of an *agal* (headrope), *kafayeh* (headcloth), *gotra* (cap), *thobe* (gown), *abaya* (cloak), and sandals. To this day we cherish a photograph of Senator Fulbright standing in our living room in Jidda clad in his new clothes drinking a martini, with Tewfik standing beside him holding a martini pitcher on a sterling silver tray.

KATHRYN K. MCNEIL

Neighbors

THE CABIN WAS RIGHT BELOW my mailbox on the county road, and I passed it every day, in the summertime, when I went up or down the mountain. For as long as I can remember, it had been empty. It was a sight, even for Appalachia. Rags were stuffed in the openings where windows had once been. The porch was packed with old lumber and broken-down furniture. The yard was scattered with bits of car parts and junk. A Maytag washer sat under a tree, rusted out, and nosed into the bank above the house was an abandoned pickup truck, its wheels removed long ago, propped up on four rocks.

My neighborhood, Hemphill, was one place in the United States where "trade-ins" ended up on the shoulder of the road, driven till the last gasp of life left them and they were abandoned to become part of the scenery. I got used to these wrecks I'd pass going up to my place, and I tried to keep my mind on the blue mountains surrounding me instead.

One spring, not so far back, driving up the mountain in my Jeep, loaded with groceries and belongings for my annual summer vacation, I passed the cabin and noticed a line of wash running from the

146

porch to a tree, and a little curl of smoke coming out of the stove pipe at the side of the house. I asked Bonnie about it when she came to help me move in. Bonnie and her husband, George, were my friends and caretakers, and they knew everything that happened in Hemphill Cove, North Carolina, this seven-mile stretch of road with small cabins and farms running alongside it, and behind them, Hemphill Creek pouring down off the mountain from higher up.

"That cabin belongs to Jamie Sutton. He's back home, out of prison," she said, unpacking the groceries and putting them on the shelf. "Served his time, I reckon. I sure hope he goes straight for a change. Trouble with Jamie is the company he keeps. Otherwise he's a good sort. George has got him a job at the sawmill."

"Bonnie, how many people has George brought to the sawmill over the years?" I could count six at least, half of them relatives. George was kind, always helping a person get back on his feet.

"Jamie's all alone now," she continued, pressing the paper bags flat and putting them in the closet. "You might have heard some years back how he found his daddy dead under his tractor, bled to death, mowing too steep a side of the pasture. It turned over on him. That was a terrible day for Jamie."

I shivered, imagining the scene. Mountain people took lots of chances, farming on steep land. They needed to make the most of what was theirs. I felt sad for Jamie.

Each time I passed his cabin now I noticed different things. He had a red chow dog that he kept on a long chain while he was at work. The yard stayed exactly the same, littered, and the cabin too, but when he was at home, no matter the temperature, the door stood open. He had placed a straight-back chair, like one out of a dining room set, on the side of the road by his mailbox. It looked very strange there, very proper, as though its owner planned to have a front seat at some event about to happen on the road.

One day I slowed down when I got to his place, just looking to see if there was anything different. It was Saturday and the door was open. I saw Jamie in the yard. He was naked to the waist, though it was still early June and cool. He waved and I waved back. On an im-

pulse—I'm old now but I still follow impulses, and he was my neighbor after all—I stopped, and rolled down the window.

"Good morning," I yelled.

"'Morning," he said, putting down the wrench he was using.

I couldn't think of anything suitable to say. "Pretty day, isn't it?"

"Yep. Mighty pretty day."

I put the car in gear again and slowly moved on. But I felt better.
It was good to slow down and not rush past, as I did so often, past
these simple little cabins, too busy with my own affairs, eager to
reach my own comfortable place and my well-fed friends waiting for
my return.

The next time Bonnie came, I told her I'd met Jamie at last. She
was helping me fold the sheets. "George says Jamie never brings any
lunch to work. Between them all at the Mill they split up their food
and there's enough for him. He tells them he's not hungry but they
give it to him anyway. It's a long time between six in the morning
when they leave and six at night when they get home." She shook
her head. "There's not much extry to eat around Jamie's, he got so
many debts to pay.

"The power people turned off his electricity several times for
not paying his bill," she continued. "That didn't stop Jamie. He just
took a meter off somone's cabin who was gone and hooked it up to
his wall. After a while they found out and slapped another fine on
him. I think he's got power now."

I thought he was mighty ingenious. "Is he a good worker at the
sawmill?"

"George says he's steady, doesn't come drunk, either. Of course
the mill wouldn't keep no one a minute if he acted the least bit
drunk. Jamie knows that and he's careful, weekdays anyways."

I was getting a picture of my neighbor.

The weeks went by and I settled in. It was late June now, and the
flame azalea along the banks above the road was blooming in all
shades of orange—about the prettiest sight one could see. Hanging
over Jamie's old pickup truck was a specially pretty one, and I slowed

down to admire it. I saw him bending over a motorcycle, working on the engine, bare to the waist as usual. He straightened up and waved. My window was down. The weather was getting warm.

"It's such a pretty color," I yelled to him, pointing to the bush. Then I pulled over by his mailbox, where the wooden chair sat. He walked over slowly.

"I'm Kathryn McNeil. It's good to see your cabin open again." We shook hands through the window. He had the bluest eyes I'd seen for awhile. He looked thirtyish, though his skin was red and rough from years of exposure and other things I could guess at. His long red hair was tied back with a rag, and it, plus his ruddiness, gave him a kind of tawny look.

"Who sits in the chair?" I asked.

"I do," and he sat down in it and crossed his legs.

I felt it was a silly question. He looked at home in it. After all, it was his chair.

"George picks me up here each morning and I just sit here and wait."

How odd, I thought, to be sitting here in the dark at six in the morning, just waiting. But at least he was ready and not keeping anybody waiting, which was more than I could say for others I knew.

"Best be on my way, I guess," I said, smiling at him. "I'm interfering with your repairs there," and I started my engine.

"Don't matter a bit," he said, sitting there still in his chair, swinging his crossed leg and looking at me.

"See you soon." I waved again and drove up the road.

I asked Bonnie the next time she came to work if Jamie would be insulted if I left him some extra food. There is always that fine line with working people living on the ragged edge. I certainly didn't want to hurt his feelings. Bonnie assured me he'd be pleased. One day while he was at work, I left half of a roasted chicken and some cooked yams in a brown bag in the yard. When I approached, the chow dog growled at me. I backed off and looked for some place near the porch but off the ground. There was an old stump with hub caps piled on it. I dumped the hub caps on the ground and put the bag there instead and wrote "Jamie" on it and my initials. I hoped no animal would get to it all those hours it would sit there. The next day when I made my trip down the mountain, I looked to see if a dog had scattered the bag around the place, but I saw no signs. Jamie must have found it. Now I knew where to take my leftover food this summer.

Almost every week I left a bag on the stump, and it was always gone when I drove by the next day. Once I left a casserole. Eventually I got it back. Jamie gave it to George who gave it to Bonnie who brought it back the next Wednesday when she came to work. Meanwhile, we kept waving to each other, Jamie and I, when I passed him on weekends. That was the extent of our connection until one Sunday afternoon when I had "callers."

I was lying in the hammock, out on the back lawn, half reading, half watching the clouds move across the mountains, when I heard a loud banging on the front door. Startled, I walked inside and peeped out the window near the front door. Jamie and another man were standing there. Jamie was dressed neatly but his companion was a stranger to me and was shirtless and groggy. Against my better instincts I opened the door.

"Mrs. McNeil, I've come to thank you," Jamie said.

His friend wavered and looked like he might be ill. I was caught at a loss. Should I visit with them outside or invite them in? Would I get them out once they came in? Jamie looked friendly and his eyes seemed bluer than ever in his red face. I held the door open.

Jamie strolled inside, looking at the beams in the high ceiling, the soft couches. His friend staggered as he followed him to the table in the window where I usually sat with visitors. The view was nice from there.

"The lady wants you to sit here, Bud," Jamie said roughly to his friend, pushing him down into a chair.

I knew I had problems. I could now see that Bud was dead drunk. He might even be sick any minute. My mind switched back and forth from how to get rid of them politely, to what I might grab to give Bud if he needed help in a hurry. His head had fallen on his chest.

What a fool I was to get caught all alone, inside, with a couple of unpredictable mountain men. I looked at Jamie. He was looking around the room admiringly, at the wall hangings from Ecuador, at the watercolors of the mountains. "How's your work going at the sawmill?" I asked him, trying to get a handle on my nerves.

"Just dandy," Jamie answered. He was slouched in his chair and didn't look like he would be moving any time soon.

It crossed my mind that I might be robbed by these two. Why not? I had so much and they, nothing. I had asked for it, stepping into this forlorn man's life with my offerings of food and bits of neighborliness.

Bud groaned, and opening his eyes, looked at me vaguely and belched. I don't know which bothered me more at that moment, the fear of being robbed or of him becoming ill. I think the latter.

Jamie leaned over and cuffed him roughly on the side of his head.

"Shut up, you fool," he said fiercely to him. "You're in the presence of a lady."

Bud groaned again and put his arm up defensively, shielding his face from another blow.

I knew then and there I was safe. Jamie wouldn't hurt me.

"I think you both better go now," I said smiling faintly at Jamie. I stood up and placed my chair carefully under the table, hoping to encourage them to stand too.

"Bud's not well," I continued, "and I don't want him here. I know you understand, Jamie." I hoped I might appeal to his sense of fitness, if such existed for him.

He stood too, after a moment. "We'll go now, Mrs. McNeil. Just wanted you to know I'm grateful for the food." They walked to the door with me, Jamie weaving a little, too, I thought. When he reached the door he opened it and with a mighty shove pushed Bud out and against the side of the house. Slowly, Bud slumped to the concrete patio, blood dripping down his face from an ugly cut where his face had hit the wall.

I stood there dumbfounded. Then Jamie dragged him to his feet, and half carrying, half pushing him, got him into the truck they'd come in. Down the road they went and disappeared out of my sight, around a curve. I continued to stand there, watching, wanting to be sure they'd keep going. I saw the truck emerge from the woods for a few seconds and disappear again around another curve. I was alone again.

The soft mountain breeze picked up and beckoned me up the hill and into the woods. I needed to walk, to think, to shed the brutality I had so recently been part of. I had glimpsed another world far away from mine.

I went away on a trip shortly after this and didn't return for several weeks. When I drove up the road, Jamie's cabin looked locked up and the chow dog was gone.

"Where's Jamie?" I asked Bonnie when she came up on her weekly visit.

She shook her head and sat down with me at the table in the window to have a cup of coffee before she started her work.

"He's back in jail," she said. "Sheriff came to the sawmill and took him away last week. Seems like he got involved in one of those insurance scams. A friend of his asked him to drive his new truck and wreck it for the insurance. I guess he's lucky he didn't get killed."

We sipped our coffee silently together looking at the mountains. What was there to say? Just beyond the porch the blue ridges stretched, one after one, as far as the eye could see.

California Landmarks

RHODA H. GOLDMAN

The Lady

WE WERE ALL IN AN ANTICIPATORY, festive mood as we entered the San Francisco Museum of Modern Art after negotiating the puddles and umbrella-balancing caused by the downpour. The main exhibit space of the museum on the fourth floor of the Veteran's Building was the location for the Valentine Ball. For some inexplicable reason, the elevator stopped at the third floor, the doors opened and closed before we proceeded to our final destination. We all had a brief glimpse of the wall opposite the elevator. That pause was enough for me to catch sight of a familiar painting, "La Femme au Chapeau" (The Woman in a Hat) by Matisse. I hadn't realized that she had moved to that spot until the museum was ready to move to its new building.

The evening was a real fête, but it was memories of that painting that I recall. I can still remember my initial impression upon viewing this work of art for the first time after my mother hung it in the living room of my parents' apartment. Mom, who had an innate sense of beauty and quality, seemed to me to have gone far astray on this one. I thought the painting was *awful*.

As I have been clearing out my parents' apartment, I see what an

acquisitive collector, albeit an eclectic one, my mother was. However, everything seemed to have a proper place, and one was more
aware of the harmonious whole rather than the individual acquisi-
tions. Perhaps this was one of the main reasons this painting didn't
fit, as far as I was concerned.

I heard the story as it unfolded, then and many times since, of
how Mom became involved in collecting Impressionist art.
Through Grammy, Mom's mother, she had become acquainted with
Sarah Stein, wife of Michael, sister-in-law of Leo and Gertrude. All
of them had lived in Paris, and had been patrons of struggling
painters—Gertrude of Picasso, and Michael and Sarah of Matisse.
This was particularly meaningful when these artists and others of
the same genre were criticized and reviled for their first exhibit in
the early 1900s. Because of the wild colors and nonrepresentational
aspects of their work, they had been called "Les Fauvres," the Wild
Beasts. As a result of their encouragement, the Steins had acquired
numerous paintings from the artists they supported.

After Michael's death, Sarah moved to Palo Alto, where I
remember going with my mother to visit her in her home. My
recollection is of a light, airy house, but I have no memory of the
artwork. Sarah and my mother became good friends. After some
years, Sarah moved to an apartment in San Francisco. She was the
sole support of her grandson, Danny, and his demands on her
were continual and immense. He had many plans and schemes,
primary among them betting the horses. He must have rarely
won! My mother only learned of this after some time, because Sarah was too proud to divulge the reason for her reduced circumstances.

Sarah went through her limited resources and then began to sell
her possessions, namely her art collection, one by one. My mother
happened to learn of this during one of their periodic phone calls.
When Sarah mentioned casually that she had sold a Matisse painting
to Frank Perls, a dealer in Los Angeles, my mother was horrified.
She finally convinced Sarah that she was getting very little money
for this prize. Immediately, my mother charged into action. She per-

suaded Sarah to stop the transaction. Next, Mom spoke to friends who were art collectors and convinced them that these valuable works should remain in the San Francisco area. When Matisse's portraits of Michael and Sarah Stein became available, she persuaded Nat Cummings of Chicago to purchase Michael's portrait as a foundation for the Michael and Sarah Stein collection at the San Francisco Museum of Art. My parents bought the one of Sarah, which hung in the front hall of their home. At that time, purchasers could promise these artworks to a museum but retain them during the benefactor's lifetime.

It was in the 1950s that my parents acquired the famous "Lady." My first reaction must have been similar to that of the Parisians when they saw what we now consider the advanced and striking work of the Impressionists.

Time does make a difference. I viewed this large brilliant canvas on so many occasions, it became familiar. I was also intrigued by my mother's explanation of the subject matter. Madame Matisse had posed, dressed entirely in black, including her large hat, except for an orange ribbon tied around her throat. She had been standing against a white fence. It did intrigue me that Matisse's eye had translated the palette of this painting into a brilliant canvas even flesh tones were dabbed with green and other vivid colors. Without my realizing it, I became tremendously attached to "The Lady."

The San Francisco Museum of Modern Art was the benefactor of a bequest from my mother of her major paintings. Mom had been active with the museum, including serving as president for many, many years. I realized the finality of her passing when the museum acquired these works of art. At a press conference in a room where the museum exhibited some of the major works of art from her collection, I saw "The Lady" hanging in the place of honor. I felt the pain of separation. Its beauty and vivid colors still reverberated for all who viewed it. To me, it will always be hanging on the pale green wall in my parents' living room. The fireplace is to the far left, and underneath is a rectangular oriental-type table of wood, dark and low. On the table to the right stands Marino Marini's sculpture of a horse, and to the left is a large, bright turquoise clay jar, also oriental. In my mind's eye, no matter where it is, this is my memory of "The Lady."

BETTY WHITRIDGE

Oh Tannenbaum

OUR SON ARNOLD'S HOUSE, with all his family's belongings, clothing, family treasures burnt to the ground just before Christmas. This left us in a mood far from festive. Decorating our own house, putting up a Christmas tree seemed frivolous, inappropriate—our hearts just weren't in it.

But ah, my toes and oh my friends, there was still the restorative twice-a-day dog walk on Crissy Field Beach in the Presidio of San Francisco. One spindly, lonely, dwarfed tree stands there in solitary sadness. Every Christmas season, whimsical souls throw bits of scruffy tinsel on this grungy caricature of a tree. Wheeee, thought I—this is something I can do to cheer myself. I can adorn *this* tree with beach flotsam to surprise and delight the daily parade. Walkers, joggers, bikers, windsurfers, fishermen, tourists, fitness freaks, hand-holding lovers, an occasional horse and rider, marching soldiers, tired housewives, devoted dog walkers, strollers, naturalists, tricycles, pass constantly in splendid procession.

Immediately my newly honed eye spots a piece of brilliant orange plastic in the sand. *Alors!* When hung on the pathetic tree, it is instantly transformed into a zingy space ship! All those white clam shells with holes are just ready and waiting to be hung. Clem, our Jack Russell (the reason for the daily-double-dog-walk) grows slightly bored with the unusual delay, a puzzling departure from the norm. But Clem is a good sport and gamely fetches and retrieves her tennis ball, which I throw between hangs. Lunchtime approaches, time to go home. During the lunch break I gather bright red yarn, tin foil, cardboard tubes, can lids, bottle tops, old keys to be strung and tied.

Later Clem announces in clear English *"The time has come* for the afternoon walk." Feeling like Queen of the Bag Ladies with my gaily tied garbage items, off Clem and I go to the beach again. We are instantly rewarded with an adorable flowered pink and white baby sandal, a purple glove, a red plastic tube, blue tangled fish netting. Armed with my trusty skein of red yarn, I fashion these gifts from the sea into, perhaps not exquisitely elegant, but surely unique Christmas tree ornaments. I am pleased as I hang them on the wimpy tree. Beauty, after all, is in the eye of the beholder. Simultaneous yarn tying, ornament hanging, tennis ball throwing in a high wind is a delicate artform and an amazing even if obscure, unheralded, accomplishment.

A gaggle of macho, muscular joggers shoots past shouting: *"Hey! Right on, lady!"* "Bring something to hang on this tree when you jog by tomorrow," I yell back. They smile and nod agreement.

A tweedy, brogan-shod Germanic frau stops to admire and photograph the tree and Clem and me in my (purely serendipitous) red warm-up suit. "Oh Tannenbaum! What a wonderful city to do this," she says in her heavily guttural foreign accent. Obviously she thinks that I am a municipally employed Christmas elf.

On our way back to our waiting auto at the end of this hanging session, Clem and I hand red tied jetsam/flotsam items to astonished walker joggers. "Tie this on the Christmas tree as you jog by," I instruct them. They look surprised but pleased and interested.

The theme of this tree is "Dog walkers clean up the beach." An ominously dire threat looms blackly: the eminent transition of the Presidio from military base to national park will eliminate all dogs.

In the evenings, I send out cards to all our dog-walking acquaintances: "Bring an ornament with your dog's name on it and hang it on the tree at Crissy Field."

Every day it gets more exciting going to the beach to see the tree. It becomes more and more glittery, festooned with all sorts and conditions of imaginatively creative ornaments. Old light globes, pieces of surf boards, many lost car keys. *Yes!* The postcards are getting through, for there are ornaments with dog's names: "Dante," "Rex," "Jo," dogs whom we know from our twice-a-day walks.

Greetings shower on me during each hanging time: "*Oh!* Are *you* the wonderful person who does this every year?" (No.) "Thank you, thank you."

"We love the tree!" sings out a group of Asian students.

"May we take your picture with the tree? We're from Florida and there is nothing like this happening there."

So far, me'n the tree 'n Clem are in photo albums in Florida, Berlin, London, and goodness knows where else.

Next cold, windy dog walk, the magical tree has sprouted endless delights—a green glove to go with my found purple one—four more blue, red, yellow plastic ballpoint pens (people seem to drop lots of ballpoint pens overboard), six additional colorful plastic cigarette holders, a sodden toy Mickey Mouse. Clem and I add the fifty yellow plastic tennis ball can lids that I scrounged at the California Tennis Club yesterday and tied with red yarn. Never mind that the club manager looked at me in a peculiar manner.

"It's beautiful! It's beautiful!" call two helmeted speeding bikers.

"Oh, Betty Whitridge, that's the funniest thing I've ever seen! You are a crazy lady," chortles another bundled-up dog-walker.

"Hey! I'm real tall, let me hang some stuff up higher for you," offers a nice, and yes, *real tall* young man.

My suggestion to lonely hearts is to hang things on a tree in a public park. I have been approached by, talked to, helped by, all sorts of people these last days, and gained many new friends.

Spurred on by these rising waves of enthusiasm, I begin to cheat a little. In a burgeoning cottage industry at home, I fashion a few non-authentic flotsam, but still garbagy-looking items for hanging. Five gold rings, "popcorn" strings from the styrofoam peanuts in the Christmas boxes. A wonderful way to dispose of plastic peanuts—I should probably send this helpful hint to *Family Circle* magazine or Martha Stewart. My Little Red Riding Hood basket bulges with inimitable creations, so off we go beachward full of happy anticipation.

But, lo! What to our wondering eyes should appear, but a truckload of rangers with gloves and bags *ripping, tearing* our precious decorations *off* the tree!

"Sally Walking Dog" (a professional dog walker who brings her six or eight charges daily) is screaming ineffectually at them: "Cease and desist! We *love* this tree!"

"It's litter," the insensitive rangers dare to say.

"No! No! Not litter," screams a new passerby. "I am an artist and what this lady is doing is *art*. Conceptual art. You musn't touch it. It should be in the newspaper."

The daily running group whose tee shirts proclaim them "The Town School Moms" trots up in formation, their voices strident with protest. "Stop! Stop! Leave our tree alone, we all love it."

"We are very short-handed here," the rangers whine.

"Exactly!" I triumphantly shout. "That is the very idea. We dog walkers and others who use and love the beach are *helping* you. We are picking up the litter, giving pleasure, making a sense of community responsibility and *fun!*"

"Yeah, but we'll just hafta come take it all down," snarled these grinches who really were trying to steal Christmas.

"No, kind sirs, I promise on my dog walker's word of honor, to come back with a plastic bag just like yours after Christmas. I'll take it all off and put it in a proper receptacle." This I vow solemnly with raised right hand.

"You just go back and tell whoever issued you that silly, ridiculous order, to rescind it immediately," demands beauteous Mar Tavertini, her red hair billowing in the wind.

"*Scrooge! Scrooge! Scrooge!*" comes a resounding bellow from a trio of joggers.

"Okay, okay, we've heard enough, we'll leave the rest on the tree," concede the youngish rangers, who are really quite nice boys.

"Well then, let me look through your garbage bags and get out my best, best, favorite pretties. Things that you have heartlessly ripped off." They sigh, they look away in embarrassment whilst I paw through and rescue. Then they hand me a peace-on-earth-good-will-to-men offering: some of their very own government-issue plastic bags in which I can collect more ornaments!

We have tested whether this Christmas tree or any Christmas tree so conceived and so dedicated can long endure on government property. A bravely fought civil war and *the people* won.

NANCY GENN

Earthquake

ON OCTOBER 9, 1989 JUST BEFORE five o'clock, my husband, Tom, had come home early from the office to change into black tie. We had a wonderful evening ahead of us; we had tickets to the opera, fine seats in a privileged location that I had bought months ago from a friend, aisle seats she inherited from her grandmother. I wore my favorite short black velveteen dress with buttons up the back, my mother's amber drop earrings, and a short jacket. I always feel good when I wear that dress.

My friend Nancy Boas was to give a lecture at the de Young Museum at six o'clock. I had been dismayed that the two events were on the same evening, but Tom gave the go-ahead to my plan of attending both. That was good of him as somewhere in between was the dinner hour, which meant we'd have to catch a quick bite to eat somewhere. However, we never discussed the details of dinner as I did not want to point out how little time we would have.

Tom could see how important Nancy's lecture was to me. I had known her for more than twenty years. Her book, *The Society of Six*, focused on painters working in the San Francisco bay area in the twenties and thirties. I looked forward to the lecture as this was not only to be informative, but also to honor her for the book and concurrent exhibition.

We were almost ready to leave the house when there was a rattle and a bang and a rattle and a bang and major jerks. Our house moved as a unit, not with the torque I remember from earthquakes in our San Francisco wood-frame house, but more like a great ship at sea. We had experienced other quakes in this concrete house built by Bernard Maybeck in the Berkeley hills. Dr. Andrew Lawson, the original owner, came to Berkeley in 1902 to establish the Geology Department for the University of California. Already a respected man in his field, he located and then mapped the San Andreas fault. The neighborhood story is that he used the name San Andreas for the fault line as that was his name in Spanish. He knew about the force of a geological disturbance and ordered his home, which sits almost directly on the Hayward fault, to be build accordingly strong. We could not have been in a safer place than at home during the Loma Prieta earthquake of 1989.

Objects fell, dishes swayed, cups clanged, an artwork in a plexi-frame on the sideboard toppled and crushed a rare Chinese ceramic, a wedding present. The worst noise came from the bathroom. I had temporarily propped a large mirror against the wall behind the toilet fifteen years ago. Now long slivers of glass sprayed across the floor. But neither of us was hurt.

After a quick look around, Tom immediately thought of my ninety-three-year-old mother next door. Was she safe? He ran across the gravel square and through the garden gate. I followed a few yards behind. There was Mother sitting quietly in her garden patio. Tom dashed into her house asking as he went, "Is everything all right?" She responded with a nod and in a confident, calm voice said, "It was nothing like the big one."

Upon occasion Mother told us stories about the San Francisco earthquake of 1906. She said she was frightened and crawled under the bed and said her prayers. "Never underestimate the power of prayer," she told us with a smile. "The Lord heard me and it stopped."

The stories I like the best are about the neighbors on Jordan Avenue. They were required to cook their meals outside in makeshift places between the sidewalk and the curb on grills made of fallen bricks. No cooking or fires of any kind were allowed inside a dwelling. The children skipped up and down the sidewalk to see what their friends and neighbors were having for dinner. While their mothers were concerned and unhappy with worry, the children enjoyed the excitement.

Mother's family was fortunate as they had moved only the year before to 72 Jordan Avenue—west of Van Ness Avenue, the important dividing line where the fire was stopped. I learned only recently that Grandfather, who was in the wholesale fruit business, which required him to be up early, was standing on the corner of Jordan and Euclid Avenues waiting for the streetcar when the quake hit. He held onto the lamp post as the street rippled with the force.

There was worry about the health needs, the water and sanitation. Schools were closed. The police could do little to stop vagrants from stealing. The city was unsafe. Charley Nicoli, a beau of Mother's in the National Guard Reserves, was called to active duty. He had orders to shoot if anyone was seen looting, but he confided to Mother years later that although he saw thefts occur, he was unable to shoot anyone. Mother went to stay with her cousin in Santa Cruz, a safe place for a little girl.

But back to the present earthquake. Tom wanted to clean up the dangerous slivers of glass on the bathroom floor and check on his Parker Street building down the hill by the Bay. I tried to dissuade him. "It will be here when we return. We need to get to San Francisco." Tom was adamant.

We turned on the radio as we drove down the hill, but few stations were on the air. The people in the Parker Street building were fine. Once an old factory, Parker Street is now offices with curtain walls of factory glass, high ceilings, and thick wooden beams which had taken the quake in stride with only creaks and groans. To our surprise there was no evidence of broken glass. A half dozen or so employees still at the Nolo Press office were startled to see us in our evening clothes and appreciative of our attention. When Tom was satisfied that all was well, it was on to the city.

Heading for the Bay Bridge on 880 we saw little traffic. Only one radio station reported, "the Cypress Freeway damaged, the Cypress Freeway collapsed," but no news about any problem on the Bay Bridge. We drove carefully as we rounded the big curve to face the toll plaza, but noticed only little cracks in the pavement where the edge had dropped a few inches and broken in a zigzag pattern. We went to the toll plaza, but then instantly knew something was wrong. There was no one to take our money, no one in any of the toll booths. It was surreal. Tom drove over to the right a few yards to ask information from two people dressed in khaki uniforms with insignia I had never seen before. "The bridge is closed. The Fifth Street ramp has collapsed on the San Francisco side." (Such is the way false rumors start, it turned out.) "Turn back over there. To the left is the turnaround." To our far left by the Toll Plaza Administration Building, an officer was directing the orderly reversal of cars that had reached the toll plaza.

Heading east I groaned and questioned in dismay, "How will we get to Nancy's lecture?" Tom, in complete command, said, "That's all right, we will take the Richmond bridge and then the Golden Gate." But by the time we crossed the Richmond Bridge, traffic was heavy. We headed south on 101, and the news reported major losses on the Cypress Freeway, the Oakland approach to the Bay Bridge. There were two news stations on the air by then. We switched back and forth, each station giving a higher and higher estimate of lives lost, which later, fortunately, turned out to be exaggerated. The usually heavy traffic in rush hour was minimized by the timing of the opening of the World Series. Hundreds of people who might have been on that elevated freeway had left work early and were safe at home or at Candlestick Park ready to witness the game.

As we crossed over the Golden Gate Bridge, we could see the fire in the Marina as it was being reported on the radio. It was dusk, and yet no light came on in the city, only the red glow from the flames. Because of a possible blackout we agreed not to go to the park, as they surely would not allow us into the museum.

On to the opera. We took the Lombard Street off-ramp. It was only sensible to stay well away from the fire area. Going past Divisadero I took a careful look up the hill to see that our friends Ann and Mike Stone's house was all right, as I was sure they would hear in Washington, D.C. about the fire in the news tomorrow and I wanted to be able to give Ann a firsthand report that all was well.

It was a slow process crossing each intersection along Lombard Street and up Van Ness Avenue, for there was no electricity to power the traffic lights. Drivers were courteous; each took their turn. No honking or snarling. As we neared the top of Van Ness, it became evident that not just the Marina but the entire city was without power.

"What are we doing here?" I asked.

"You are just now asking that question?" Tom said.

I was thrilled, nonetheless, to be there. San Francisco was my city. It had had another quake. It was doing well. The people were behaving with dignity and dispatch. After three generations of family history in this town, this was where I belonged.

A young sailor in uniform, his white hat cocked forward on his head, stood in the middle of the California and Van Ness intersection directing traffic. This fine young volunteer was in command. He will always be a symbol for me of the spirit of that night.

It was evident from the dark facade of the Opera House that there was to be no performance. Our next step that night was to go by the office of Wallace, Roberts, and Todd on Second Street just south of Market to see if our daughter needed a ride to Berkeley. The barman in the neighboring building told us all were safe, and the people had left. The old four-story brick structure had held up well in the violent quake.

Meanwhile the radio dispatches increased. People from the East Bay were directed to the Embarcadero for emergency transportation. The Bay Bridge was closed; it was finally confirmed that a section on the Oakland side had collapsed. Ferry boats would take people to Oakland. We were surprised to see how large the crowd was standing in line on the dock. The multitude of people talking quietly were calmly waiting, the dark water glistening in the moonlight.

We headed for home traveling the length of California Street to reach the approach to the Golden Gate Bridge in the avenues. As signal lights were out, motorists continued being thoughtful, taking turns in an orderly fashion. At Lake Street the bridge approach narrowed to one lane. A piece of the pavement had fallen away, causing a minor backup. We crossed the bridge and retraced our route via the Richmond Bridge to Berkeley.

The headlines in the newspapers the next morning were dramatic. Our children in the north and on the east coast had stayed up half the night watching as the television reports multiplied and became increasingly exaggerated. Wild reports flashed around the globe. I telephoned Tom's brother Jerry in Vienna to assure him we were safe. His secretary, Mrs. Schneider, took the call.

"What!" she said in an excited high voice. "You went to San Francisco after the earthquake?"

"Oh yes, Mrs. Schneider," I said. "We had tickets to the opera."

RHODA H. GOLDMAN

A Moment in Time

IN ANOTHER DAY, RICHARD and I would be heading back to San Francisco. This was the last night we'd be having dinner at our Lake Tahoe home. During our stay, the mornings had mostly calm water and clear skies. There'd been few cloudy days during this month of August, but today had been one of them. It was a still night, however, and we had been able to eat our last supper on the deck.

There had been waves of family visiting us over the last three weeks. John's gang spent only a long weekend but have already put in their bid for a visit of a week next year. The next group was our daughter Susan, her husband, and three kids, immediately followed by Lisa and Doug with the twins and Jennifer. We usually sat down to eat with seven at the table, though it was only six when Aaron, Jessica, and their parents were there. When friends came to visit the number increased precipitously. I was looking forward to returning to "adult life" once more. This evening, though, I had become nostalgic. Thinking back, I found this usually happens when I am about to depart from the lake.

I'd really been upset when Dick had announced that we had the opportunity to buy this property in 1969. The last thing I wanted to worry about was another home. He kept telling me it was merely an investment and we could just hold on to the land—Ha!

Howard Friedman, married to my first cousin Phyllis, had been roaming around the lake, primarily on the Nevada side, looking for some property the two of them could acquire. Unbeknownst to me, my husband had said, "If you find something more than you want, let me know." This investigation all stemmed from the fact that my father and my uncle Dan Koshland, Phyllis's father, had turned down some beautiful property near Cascade Beach that was offered to them by Edward Heller. Besides the lot that Howard finally found, it seemed there was another available lot next door. It turned out to be approximately two and a half acres that were held in a trust for a minor child. Richard made an offer, answered by a counter-offer, and the deal was done. In the course of this acquisition, we became the owners of four hundred feet of beachfront and Phyllis and Howard, three hundred. It lies one mile south of Glenbrook, Nevada, in a small subdivision called Cedarbrook.

It didn't last as virgin territory very long. Howard was the architect for both homes and we had the same contractor, Jack Franklin. Our programs were the same—a small, easy-upkeep house with two bedrooms. However, because of the topography for each site, the houses are completely different. Ours is suspended on large hollow concrete pillars and has a wonderful overlook of the lake and the mountains behind the California side. It is the shape of a somewhat flattened V, which produces magnificent scenic outlooks but also creates angles in every room. Now, all building is regulated by the Tahoe Regional Planning Agency, which finally allowed us to add on two small bedrooms and two tiny baths two years ago. While going through this process, we found that we would never have been allowed to build in the first place if all the current regulations had been in place then, as we are on what they call "spring sensitive land," the most protected type of property. This was a surprise, though we had been very diligent about leaving boulders, rocks, and as many trees as we could—the suspension of the actual house had allowed for this.

This is a long way around of saying that now I dearly love being there, though I find it physically taxing. The air is wonderful, the surroundings beautiful and peaceful, and if I didn't have to keep house, spending a large portion of my time marketing and then cooking, it would be perfect for a retreat. Richard adores being there and I can understand that.

This particular night I was making my own farewell to Tahoe for the summer of 1995. I sat out on the deck and watched a magnificent sunset. The sun had just gone down behind the opposite peaks. The clouds above turned from a bright yellow reflection to orange into pale red as the hills started to darken to deep purple. The clouds slowly lost their bright coloration, becoming first the palest of pink and then intensifying in color, darkening and finally fading into night. What caught my eye, besides this beautiful panorama, lay to the left where there was what appeared to be a small valley, at the bottom of which could have been liquid sunshine—a pool of golden shimmering fluid. The light around this was intense, going from a bright yellow-gold to orange, to red orange, to red crimson. The thought that struck me was, "Is this what the Elysian fields look like?" It seemed that this special light and brightness lasted longer than anything else around it.

I sighed as the chilliness of evening and the darkness of night descended. I returned back to the mundane, having said goodbye to my Tahoe.

Editors' note: Rhoda died on February 17, 1996, never to return to her beloved lake.

Getting On

BABS WAUGH

Bodies

THE RADIO BLASTS DICK AND ME out of a sound sleep and he turns sleepily toward me and slings a long, bare thigh across my hip bones. "You're closest to the door," he says. "Why don't you just get up and close it." The door is our "window" because the picture window in the bedroom doesn't open. We go to sleep every night with a breeze from the west blowing in through the door across our faces. I do his bidding, getting up in the cold to close it, then get back into bed under the feathers, as Dick calls our duvet, and we lie entwined, listening to a reporter describe last night's terrorist attack on the West Bank. This morning will not be leisurely for it is Wednesday, and we have exercise class, and we must get to the center by 7:30.

We are a class of seventy-five, most of whom are cardiac patients, the rest wives. Most are men in their sixties, seventies, or eighties, with a scattering of women, some of whom are cardiac patients themselves. Our leader, Susan, a handsome white-haired woman of fifty with the build of a greyhound and perfect posture, kids with some of the men as she motions energetically for everyone to "take a giant step forward; I took a shower this morning," then laughs uproariously at her own joke. "She's so full of energy, she makes me tired," says Joan, a newcomer and another one of the wives, as am I. Dick has been a member since his angioplasty seven years ago; the group has been going for some twenty years. A staff of cardiac nurses are in attendance and defibrillators are available at all times.

Susan makes an announcement in a voice that carries over the roar of the heaters turned up to take the early-morning chill off the gym. "Ollie would like to have visitors now for ten minutes at a time," she says. I turn to the man next to me and ask him what's wrong with Ollie. "He's terminal," he says. "Cancer. Wonderful guy." I struggle to place Ollie, as I think of the irony of the situation; if your heart doesn't get you, something else will. "Actually, we're all terminal," he continues cheerfully. "Do you know what a flight pattern is?" he asks, and then explains that planes waiting to land at an airport circle at different levels in a prescribed flight pattern. I recall that he was a pilot in the war. "We're all in a flight pattern," he says "just waiting to land." I don't feel like that, I think, but then I haven't had a heart attack.

Susan signals for the tape to be turned on and we begin to warm up as "Chattanooga Choo-Choo" blasts out over the loudspeakers. After fifteen minutes we find our pulses and count for ten seconds. Hmm, I think, it's up to nineteen; that's good. Though most of the class now makes for the stationary bikes, Dick among them, I put on my jacket and head outdoors, where I walk for thirty minutes with several other women, around and around the covered pathways of the old middle school that is now the Jewish Community Center where we meet. One of the nurses has wheeled a defibrillator outdoors and walks with us for a few minutes, then leaves us to walk with one of the men, and I hear her ask about his angina pain.

Finally, it's time to go in so we straggle through the double doors back into the gym, collect mats and weights from the cupboard in the corner, and claim a space on the floor. I gaze around at my fellow classmates. Most of the men are gray-haired and some have potbellies, but a surprising number are slim and vigorous looking. We all wear shapeless warm-ups or sagging sweats; there is not a leotard among us. From what I have gathered in snatches of conversation as I walk or bicycle with one or another of them, they are typical of the Peninsula—retired Stanford professors, CEOs of technical companies, engineers, a lawyer or two and a doctor. Most were in the war—World War II, of course—and the stories they tell are often war stories. They tell only the bare bones of their stories, but as they speak, I imagine the rest, and I wonder if anything that has happened to them since the war has seemed as exciting.

The group has gathered and Susan is ready to begin. "We have a birthday boy with us today," she shouts, as she drags a grinning, embarrassed-looking participant forward and we all belt out "Happy Birthday," several of the men harmonizing at the end. We begin the next series of exercises standing and follow Susan's lead as she counts, working on our upper bodies with our weights in hand until our shoulders burn. "Now, take your little self down to your mat," she says, "and give yourself a hug." We obediently coil up on our backs, hugging our knees to our chests, then rotate our feet first clockwise, then counterclockwise, and I imagine that we look like a collection of dying bugs, their legs waving in the air. We walk our feet to the ceiling and stretch our hamstrings. Next it's the abs, a pelvic tilt, more abs, and a stretch. "You'll all have buns of steel," shouts Susan in encouragement, and then it's time for a minute of relaxation. "Close your peepers and take a deep breath clear down into your little belly," says Susan. "I take poetic license," she adds, and I hear a few guffaws. On order we reach over, find our pulses, and at the command "go" begin to count. Ah, back down to eleven, I say to myself, then hear the welcome release. "Upty-up," says Susan. "When you're up you're up, kids. Have a great day!" and we struggle up from the comfort of the floor and head out the door.

During the five years I have been coming to exercise class with Dick, I have grown fond of Susan and her seemingly endless store of enthusiasm. An R.N. herself, she has been working in the field of exercise rehabilitation for twenty years. She is the one who keeps track of us all—the one who will call Dick if we haven't been to class for a while to make sure he is all right, who will visit an ailing member in the hospital, who will bring a get-well card to class and collect the signatures. I admire the men and women in the class, too, who have in common their frightening brush with their own mortality. At every session, I notice one or two sitting on a chair near the nurses' station, looking vulnerable as a nurse bends over with her stethoscope, and I realize that some are quite fragile.

After breakfast and the paper, I jump into the shower to get ready for the day, then stand naked for a moment in front of the full-length mirror and take stock. Small breasts, one smaller than the other with the scar of a lucky biopsy, nipples, with the cold, as prominent as they ever get—they tend to be the kind that retract—a suggestion of a waist, hips fuller than I'd like but not bad, inner thighs touching at the top. I reach around behind and pull them taut and wish they looked like that. Legs serviceable; a pity, though, that I didn't get my mother's ankles, but at least my legs are long. All in all, front view not bad. Side view not so good. I pull in my stomach and resolve to do seventy abs at home on odd days when we have no class, then hold up the hand mirror and inspect my back. Nice smooth upper back; buttocks from the rear, definitely not trim. Must lose five pounds. I put on underpants and a bra and decide to groom my toenails. As I lean over, my foot on the edge of the toilet, I catch sight of the skin of my upper arm hanging loose and crepey and focus quickly on my toenails, trying not to look at my arm.

There is a gentle tap on the door and I say "Come in." Dick enters, looks pleased, bends over and kisses my back just below my bra. "I just love you," he says, as he puts his arms around my waist to give me a backward hug, his hands now cupping my bra-covered breasts, and I wonder how he can be so pleased with my aging body. "You've kept your figure," he says. "That's what I like," and I laugh and say, "You should have seen me at thirty." And he says, "Well, you should have seen me at twenty-five," and I turn around and kiss him and feel his penis swell against my body.

I continue with my toilet and Dick busies himself brushing his teeth. On my seventieth birthday last summer, I asked for and received a fancy magnifying mirror that swings out from the wall at face height. Beth, my friend since college and an artist, was a surprise guest at my birthday dinner and when I opened my present from Dick, she said, with an artist's perception, "That's a wonderful present for a seventieth. We must see things as they are."

As I look in my magnifying glass and examine the area around my eyes for smudged eye-liner, I'm not so sure. I see that in the last few years, the little fine lines have turned to major crevices. My Aunt Edna used to call them character lines. "I've earned them," she would say firmly. I must try to think that mine are character lines, too, for surgery is out. My first husband, John, frightened me out of any thought of a face-lift with tales of face-lifts-gone-wrong in patients of others he cared for. Should his opinions still affect me, I wonder, as they so often have throughout my two years as a widow and these past five years married to Dick? Then I decide in this case at least, yes, for his medical judgment was good.

My eyebrows and eyelids taken care of, I turn to the mirror over the sink and my face returns to its unmagnified self. Much better, I think, and smile to make the lines recede further. Must do that more often, I say to myself, and then I remember seeing myself on television a few years ago and thinking, she's someone I'd really like to know. I resolve to keep that positive thought in mind.

The hours of the day race by. I attack the paper pile on my desk, go out for groceries, make a few phone calls, then cook a good, speedy dinner, my years of experience paying off. Dick does the dishes as I put the food away and dry the pots and pans and we continue our dinner-table conversation about the book we have both just read (to my delight, he likes to read an occasional novel, too), and then we sit for an hour or so in the living room, reading. When I realize I have nodded off over my book, I announce that I am going to bed. I complete my bedtime ablutions, then wide awake again snuggle under the feathers and continue to read. I hear Dick coming down the hallway toward the bedroom, put my book aside, and admire him silently as he comes slouching into the bedroom in his good-looking sweater and slacks. A friend said to me recently about Dick, "My grandmother would have said that he 'cuts a fine figure,'" and we chuckled together at the aptness of her quaint phrase.

I examine his tall, lean body, grown familiar in the five years we have been married, as he methodically strips down to his shorts, then disappears into the bathroom, to reemerge in a dark-blue nightshirt which hits him just below the knees, and which I find strangely masculine, in a Roman toga sort of way. I admire his legs as he takes off his watch and his glasses, pulls down his shorts, flips them onto the chair with his foot, then walks around the end of the bed to open the door. It's his face I really love, though, I think: his nice, studious look, his intelligent eyes, alert and, I realize, slightly magnified through his glasses, his mouth with the beginning of a crooked smile as he tells one of his long, growing-up-in-Fayetteville, Arkansas, stories. If I wake in the morning before he does, I like to look at his profile on the pillow next to mine, at the shape of his mouth in repose and the smile crinkles in the corner of his eyes. He's talking now about something he's just read as he rounds the bed once again, climbs into his side, turns off his light, and pulls me close. I am his hot-water bottle as we lie curved together, his arms icy around my middle just for the first few seconds, my buttocks cupped by his nether regions. "I'll smooth your feathers," he says as he strokes my thigh and I feel a good-night kiss on my right shoulder and I feel safe—from what I'm not quite sure. We're both sleepy now—the morning may be our time to frolic—and we settle down quietly, our legs entwined, my mind at rest. I am still surprised that I can go to sleep this way, but I do, Dick's body, warm and comforting, curved around mine. Sometime during the night, unaware, we turn away from each other and sink into our separate selves. In the last few years, we have begun to be in each other's dreams, but for the most part, our dreams are furnished with people from our separate pasts.

The next morning, Dick's hand may brush my left nipple and I'll come suddenly alive to his caresses, amazed that such pleasures are still within reach. Our children and grandchildren would be surprised and probably embarrassed by our sex life, unathletic as it is, even that we have one at all at our advanced ages. We think they suspect. We'll leave it at that.

JOANN REINHARDT

The Cold Sore

IN THE SPRING OF 1967, my father asked my brother and sister and me to go to San Marino for a week to our old home to sort through and divide up the family possessions. Daddy had decided to sell the house and would be moving nearby to my brother's family. Our mother, as a result of a series of strokes, was in a nursing home. By then I had given up the idea that by sheer will I could make her better, make her respond, that just seeing me would make her focus and say, "Well hello, dear. I'm so glad to see you." Like in a TV show, or something. Just months before, her doctor had told me, "You must realize your mother isn't going to get any better," because I kept asking, "Can't someone do something?" The answer was no.

What we feared would be a sad and dreary week turned out to be a happy one. My older sister, Ruthie, and I stayed in Mother's old room. Her clothes were still in the closet and in the dresser. On top of the dresser scarf were the bottles and combs and pictures from our childhood. A small framed photograph of my father in his World War I uniform was there, and on the wall nearby, a picture of Mother in her twenties with marcelled hair and wearing a chiffon sleeveless dress, posed with her three children: my brother in a white sailor suit, my sister, adorable in polka-dot organdy, and I a smiling baby on Mother's lap. Being in that room somehow softened the reality we were facing.

Every morning Ruthie and I set the alarm for seven o'clock. By April, the sun was streaming through the wooden Venetian blinds onto the blue and white wallpaper—blue was Mother's favorite color—and we quickly made our beds with the white candlewick spreads. Mother hated an unmade bed.

By the time Ruthie and I got to the kitchen to have breakfast, Daddy had already been up for an hour and was entertaining and being entertained by my six-year-old son, Andy, who had come with me on the trip. My husband Dick thought he could cope with the two older boys while I was away, but not with all three. It was Andy who first noticed my cold sore on our second day in San Marino.

"Mommy, what's that thing on your lip?" he asked.

"Just a little cold sore," I replied. "It'll go away soon."

We went through Mother's things first. Daddy said, "Let's give everything away. If by some miracle your mother recovers, we'll go out and buy everything new."

Mother didn't have many clothes and wasn't interested in fashion. She wore blue jeans and plaid shirts for housework and gardening and changed in the afternoon into a dress. She always wore a girdle and stockings. A girdle made her feel better, she said.

Every afternoon at about four o'clock my brother arrived at the house from his job as a high school history teacher. We sat in the sun room talking, choosing books from Daddy's bookshelves, making choices about who would get the silver tea service and the quilts from the cedar chest and the mahogany twin beds.

"Mean-looking cold sore you've got there," my brother said sympathetically, since he, too, sometimes got them.

"Well," I said, "I think it will get better soon. Probably the sun, or maybe stress."

Actually, it didn't seem to be getting better. It seemed to be getting worse. The cold sore was spreading out across my upper lip.

After Ruthie and I went through Mother's room we started on our own rooms. I went through boxes of letters from old boyfriends. In the ninth grade I had my first real boyfriend, and he and I wrote a letter every school night and dropped it into the other's locker before school the next morning. I still remember the thrill of finding that neatly folded piece of binder paper waiting for me when I opened my locker. There were other letters from girlfriends and boyfriends and many letters from Columbia University and Europe from a boy named Dick Reinhardt. I had boxes of school projects and notes and bluebooks. My baby doll, Sally, was still there but my Shirley Temple doll and a dark-haired doll named Elizabeth, which I had given to my nieces years before, had disappeared long ago. My red ukulele from Stanford was there and so were a lot of old art projects and dried up oil paints and crumbled pastels and stiff brushes that were remnants of an era when I seemed to have more time for myself. I decided to save just one boxful of special things—my Willkie button collection, my autograph book, some school pictures, and my baby doll.

We all, even Daddy, found old treasures. One afternoon when my brother was there, we sat down with Old Fashioneds—Mother's favorite drink—and Daddy read aloud letters to him from Herbert Hoover and Henry James, the nephew of *the* Henry James, and others whom he had worked with on the Danube River Commission after World War I. He was so moved by the letters that he decided he couldn't throw them away after all. He got out his old uniform with his heavy officer's hat. (He always said it was the hat that made him bald.) He showed us his puttees and something called his musette bag, a World War I version of a dop kit. He decided not to throw those away, either.

Ruthie and I usually cooked dinner, working effortlessly together in the kitchen. We cooked on the old gas stove with Mother's seasoned iron skillets and nesting heavy saucepans, and warmed the plates as she used to do on top of the oven, which rose above the stove at shoulder height. We fixed food that we knew Daddy liked and he was very happy to have us there. He said, "Jo, I'm sorry you didn't have any daughters," and I burst into tears and said I was sorry too, but sons were also pretty nice. I was surprised at how close to the surface the tears were.

The cold sore kept growing, inching toward my nose. We joked about it now. I had to mention it when friends and neighbors stopped by, just to make sure they knew it wasn't permanent. Andy looked at me as if he thought it might be. On the day before we were to leave, Daddy took us to lunch at the Colonial Kitchen on Huntington Drive where he and Mother had liked to go.

I put makeup on the cold sore, which by now was up to one nostril, and I felt it improved the look a little. I spent the entire lunch with one finger casually under my nose with my fist obscuring my upper lip, as if I were thinking very seriously about something. It made eating difficult but I managed.

On the last day, Ruthie's husband drove down from their home in Stockton with a second car, and we packed up the portable treasures. Daddy would send the rest by van. Ruthie and I started out about five in the afternoon, thinking nervously about doing the Ridge Route in darkness. Daddy stood on the driveway, wearing his faded Balboa blues and a blue denim shirt, one hand on his hip, leaning slightly backwards with a big smile on his still-handsome face. I have that picture in my mind like a photograph. In fact, that was the last time I saw him. He died suddenly in June of that year.

Since that week in 1967 I have never had another cold sore that equaled that one. I also haven't had to clear out my childhood home, believing that we were all having a good time because we were laughing so much.

JEAN GANSA

About Valerie, Sina and Martin, Alex and Me, and No More

THERE, LOOMING TO THE RIGHT, is the Santa Monica Pier. I notice it right away as Alex and I walk out onto the beach for the first time in three years. "Let's go see if Valerie is there," I say. "Finally I think I am ready." Alex solemnly nods. We turn and walk toward the pier.

Valerie had been a waitress at the Boathouse, a restaurant on the pier. I hope she still is. For ten years Alex and I had taken Sina and Martin, his mother and stepfather, to lunch or dinner there on our visits. We would come down from San Francisco where we live—exactly 448 miles north of Los Angeles where Sina and Martin lived. The reason I know the exact mileage is that we would often drive down and it's a long way, especially for a weekend.

After Alex and I had been married for a couple of years we began to do this regularly. At that time Sina was eighty-two and Martin was eighty-three years old. We stopped after Martin died at the age of ninety-two and Sina moved up to San Francisco to live with us for what turned out to be the last year of her life.

Before I tell you more about Sina and Martin let me tell you about Valerie. She was a slim, attractive blond woman in her middle thirties when we first met her in 1984. Valerie impressed us over the years with her friendliness and patience. On a typical visit we would arrive at the restaurant and wait in line for "our" table—the one against the windows looking out onto the beach and ocean.

Holding Sina by the elbow, Martin would move her very slowly to the table. They were a rarity in the Boathouse Restaurant. Martin stood tall and erect, old sea captain that he was; his eyes were the color of the ocean on a sunny day, his hair thick and white. Quite stiff in his eighties, he rather shuffled along. He had grown a beard when shaving became difficult for him. His childhood had been spent on an island off Estonia before he came to the United States at the time of the Russian Revolution. He always wore a hat, often a beige floppy rain hat which matched the one worn by Sina. She was very bent over with osteoporosis and had shrunk to barely five feet tall. She too had bright blue eyes, a very long and thin face with the beautiful fair skin of people from the northern countries, for she had grown up in Latvia. She always wore a dress and a hat and carried her purse even though by then it had no money in it.

After reaching the booth with its chrome-edged table and paper placemats, they took time deciding what to eat. Martin didn't hear well and that added more time. This was not a leisurely, elegant restaurant. There was a sometimes very noisy bar on the ocean side with a TV showing the latest football or other sport event. Other patrons, couples in their thirties or families with young children, tended to wear shorts and other casual beach wear. A sign on the door read, "No Bare Feet or Bathing Suits." Not only were Sina and Martin probably the oldest people who ever went to the restaurant, but so were Alex and I—then in our middle fifties.

People tended to eat and come and go rather quickly, but Valerie never gave us the feeling that we were slowing things down. She would stand there waiting for our order with either a smile on her face or a really interested look in her hazel eyes, sometimes leaning way over to hear what Sina was saying, other times waiting very patiently while Alex and I tried to get Sina to decide what she wanted or tried to get her to want something. She didn't have much of an appetite. Martin, on the other hand, had no problem with his appetite and usually ordered red snapper. When the restaurant was very busy as it often was, it would take Valerie ten minutes or more to get to us, much to Martin's irritation which he made no effort to hide. She always apologized, saying something like, "Oh, I know, I know" to Martin's expression of disgruntlement and then looking very interested in what we might want.

Over the years Alex and I and Valerie would ask each other questions about our respective lives. Occasionally one, two, or three of Alex's sons came with us. Later Valerie would want to know about their lives. We learned that Valerie had a steady boyfriend and she showed us photographs from a trip to Costa Rica where they had gone scuba diving—but that was about all we knew. There must have been times when she was not at the restaurant, but I don't remember them. As I reminisce about Valerie, I think she learned far more about us than we did about her. Or is it just that I forgot? It doesn't occur to me that she may have forgotten anything about us.

Why did we go to the Boathouse Restaurant? After Martin retired he loved to visit the ocean when he could and drove out there from their home in central Los Angeles. At the age of eighty-four he gave it up—partially as the result of an accident which miraculously did not kill him but put him in the hospital for several weeks, and kept him from driving for several months. The other miracle is that it was not his fault. Martin drove as though he were still the captain of a huge ship for which all others would automatically move over should he want to change lanes. His deafness didn't help.

One reason Alex and I first started to drive down was to avoid the terror of being picked up at the airport by Martin. In this accident Martin's life was saved by his beautifully preserved 1956 gray bomb of a Pontiac. Sadly for Martin the car was not repairable. He had no intention of not driving again and it took several years of fast talking on our side and slow repair on the part of the car repair shop to achieve our goal of a safer life for all. The shop was two blocks away from Martin and Sina's house and he would often go visit his car, which was sitting on the lot in back of the shop. The frame was bent and we were told it was basically unrepairable but Martin kept hoping. Several years later, the shop closed and Martin gave us permission to sell the car.

After that he would ride the bus down Wilshire Boulevard in Los Angeles, which took an hour and a half to reach the beach in Santa Monica. After a bad fall on the bus he had to give this up too. So his trips to the beach were limited to our visits. A walk down the Santa Monica Pier had always been a part of his trips, and perhaps he was the one to introduce us to the Boathouse Restaurant. I'm not sure. The Santa Monica Pier was located close to the end of the bus line Martin used to ride and the only pier for miles around. There was a very old rounded sign above the bridge which was lit up at night. After walking down the bridge you would see various carnival-like games on the left, including the little cars that you can drive around and bump into others. It was all rather seedy looking, but at the end of the pier there were fishermen fishing, sea gulls diving, and a view out to the horizon. That must have been the place Martin loved to go. The Boathouse was the only restaurant on the pier.

It was still important to have a walk to the end of the pier. Sina loved to look and smile at all the children who could be found there—but not the tall teenagers who zoomed around on roller skates with loud stereos. Martin still loved to be at the end of the pier and gaze at the ocean. As we walked along the pier, people, especially those of Chicano and Asian background, would smile at Sina and Martin—this very old couple with their old children.

Sina and Martin's house was located on Commonwealth Avenue, just a few blocks off Wilshire Boulevard near Bullocks department store and The Town House, a once-elegant hotel—both now abandoned. The neighborhood had been one of mostly middle-class white families. Now their house and the one next door were the only single-family houses left. All the rest were torn down and replaced by parking lots and various-sized apartment houses. The neighbors were mostly Korean and Chicano and ads for vacancies in the apartment next door were written in Korean—a way to ensure Korean tenants I assume.

Homeless men wandered the streets, slept in the backyard, and ate the fruit off the trees. The noise of helicopters overhead was a normal sound in the night along with the early-morning songs of the many birds who crowded the garden. There were virtually no other gardens left for them to sing in.

This had been Alex's home since his early teens. Several years after his father died, Sina married Martin and they had lived there ever since despite years of urging by Alex to move nearer us in San Francisco. Martin loved his garden and Sina seemed to go along with what he wanted to do—I'm not sure what she really wanted. After a stint in the hospital for the fracture of a vertebra in which her doctor loaded her up with several warring medications before Alex and I could get there, Sina never recovered her adult thinking abilities. She absolutely adored her son Alex. Whenever I would ask her what she would like to do, she would always give a big smile and respond with, "Whatever Alex is doing." She had a basically loving nature and she and I got along well—particularly when we were both being devoted to Alex's well-being.

Over the years when Alex and I came to visit, there would be a crisis of one kind or another: a trip to the emergency room, our finding out that Sina and Martin had fired yet another Polish helper whom we had hired on the previous visit, then finding and hiring another helper, Alex searching the house for the mail, writing checks, and getting Martin to sign them before the phone or the water or the electricity was disconnected, or discontinued, or my buying another tea kettle to replace the last one, which had burned out after being forgotten on the stove.

So our visits to the Santa Monica Pier were a welcome treat for all of us. Martin would sing, "My Bonnie lies over the ocean" from the back seat with me while Sina would read off the names of the streets and stores as we passed them from the front seat with Alex. Or she would tell Alex to drive carefully and to take care of himself as he must really be too tired to drive. Then Martin would call out from the back seat, "Don't spare the horses."

When we reached the Boathouse Restaurant Valerie would welcome us so warmly that we all relaxed. There was a lovely view of the beach and the ocean and when Martin got restless he could get up and start his walk down the pier. One of the dear things about Martin was that he always insisted on paying, however much Alex and I would look with horror as he pulled out a huge roll of bills and counted them off loudly. Alex thought that he had been accustomed to paying his seamen in this way. We were amazed that he didn't have his money stolen more often than he did. Walking around with a large roll of bills was very important to Martin's sense of well-being.

As Alex and I continued to visit the Santa Monica Pier and the Boathouse, we realized that part of the job of the trip was seeing Valerie and catching up with her. There would be times when someone was sick or in the hospital and we couldn't go and Alex and I would think that Sina or Martin would never get back to the pier again. Then they would recover and back we would go and Valerie would be there to greet us.

In the spring of 1991 Martin got weaker. He and his doctor seemed to hate each other. The doctor had no bedside manner and no sympathy for a frightened old man who couldn't hear. Martin didn't want to go to see him. If we were not there, appointments were broken. The doctor finally began sending Martin letters about what to do, which we could then read—a good idea. Even so, communication was not good. Finally, Martin ended up in the hospital for the last time. We flew down early one morning from San Francisco but it was too late and Martin had died in the night. Alex still can't forgive himself or the doctor for not having made the correct diagnosis. I keep trying to remind him that Martin was ninety-two years old, his quality of life had deteriorated, he didn't make it easy for the doctor to see him and perhaps he didn't want to live any longer. Alex will hear me and agree, but later he goes back to those same feelings. We really miss Martin.

After Martin died there were lots of things to do—a house to sell, to empty of almost fifty years of accumulated furniture, clothes, papers, mementoes, and moving Sina and her two cats to San Francisco. So we never got to the Boathouse. When I even thought about going there and telling Valerie that Martin had died, tears would fill my eyes and I'd think, "I just can't do it."

Six months later when I was out of town, Alex went down to Los Angeles to visit his sons and they all went out to the Boathouse. Alex told Valerie about Martin's death and she cried. I cried when Alex told me about it and I was relieved that I hadn't been along. Then a year later Sina died at our house.

Now it is almost a year after Sina's death. We are in Santa Monica for Alex's eldest son's wedding. We are staying in a hotel right on the beach. We decide to go for a walk the afternoon after the wedding. We step out onto the beach and there in the distance to the right is the pier. I finally feel that it is time to tell Valerie about Sina's death and Alex agrees. We turn north along the beach, climb up the stairs to the pier, and walk through the parking lot where we had always parked with Sina and Martin. It all looks exactly the same. After we cross the lot and the pier, we step into the restaurant. As we are doing all this I feel very hollow and kind of fluttery inside and wonder does Valerie still work here? If she does, is she here today? If she is here will I fall apart? If she's not here will I be disappointed? I decide I will be disappointed if she is not here and that I probably will cry if she is but I will not totally break down.

So here we are, Alex and I, in the restaurant looking to see if Valerie is also. There is Valerie over to the right taking an order with that same intent listening expression on her face that we had always noticed. She looks just the same, except that her blond hair is now in one long pigtail. A man whom we hadn't seen before comes over and asks if he can help us. One of us says that we would like to speak to Valerie. I feel kind of embarrassed—we aren't asking for a place to sit and eat—but he says in a very kindly, matter-of-fact way he will tell Valerie that we want to see her. We watch him wait quietly beside Valerie while she smiles and talks to the people in the same friendly patient way that she had treated us. Finally—it seems to take a long time for her to finish with the order—she comes over and gives us each a hug. Alex says, "We wanted to tell you that my mother has died." Tears fill her eyes and mine. Alex quickly says, "We are down for my son Alex's wedding." Our tears dry up. She apologizes for the tears and says, "I am glad there is a wedding being celebrated." She also tells us that she had been very close to her boss and that he recently died also. We chat some more and she wants us to stay for a meal. We say we will come back. She needs to return to her job and we leave.

As we walk back down the beach Alex says, "I shouldn't have added the part about Alex's wedding so fast." I don't say anything— just squeeze his hand. Inside I agree with him and I also know how easy it is to try to run away from the pain of really feeling the feeling of no more. Never will we take Sina and Martin anywhere again.

I think I can go back to the Boathouse for another meal with Valerie now but it makes me feel sad to think of it. It will be just Alex and me and then...someday...just one of us—if that one of us can bear it.

ROSEMARY PATTON

The Library

IT WAS, OF COURSE, THE BOOKS. We, that is my three sisters and brother and I, always knew that when the day came to dismantle our mother Ruth's apartment in San Francisco, the greatest challenge would lie in sorting through, dividing, and disposing of her library. Never mind the antiques from both sides of her family and both sides of the Atlantic, already diminished by earlier distributions as she down-sized from houses to apartments, or the boxes of family silver that, in recent years, she had so often urged us to take off her hands. Nor could we have imagined what it would mean to go through the drawers, boxes, and steamer trunks of letters, diaries, memorabilia, and photos that limned her life from girlhood to the present.

Much of the collection lies around my study, awaiting the day when I have the leisure and fortitude to read, sort, and absorb. We allowed a limited selection of these treasures to go off with my mother to North Carolina in July, and my sisters each squirrelled away yet more of her life in their suitcases as they flew back to their homes in Boston and North Carolina. Even our brother John, unable to put in an appearance, received his share. But it was the books that wore our minds and bodies, emotions and patience raw and thin.

My mother's decision to move back to Southern Pines, North Carolina, to give herself over to the attentive care of an Episcopalian retirement community after nearly thirty years in her beloved San Francisco, was precipitous. She was suddenly ready for full-time assistance—no cooking, no housekeeping—and some companionship without venturing far from home. My mother has been making startling decisions on short notice for most of her eighty-nine years. How could we possibly have been surprised?

But would we be up to the task? There was a life to reorganize in a couple of months. This time our fiercely independent, long-widowed mother no longer had the stamina to make yet another move on her own. Worse, where she was going there would be no space to hide the trunks and boxes of papers. Most crucial, a library of over five thousand volumes would not fit into two rooms.

In late March she made the decision to move. In April she was offered a suite, to be ready by mid-July. Ruth was raring to go, excited about her new adventure. As the only San Francisco daughter, I had to swing into action fast. Appraisers, antique dealers, silver merchants trooped through first, their names gathered from friends on Marin hikes, at Parachutist Book Club meetings, on the phone and over dinner. Blessings on all those good friends. It looked as though I would be on my own as I made appointments, weighed offers, and talked to siblings about who would want specific pieces of this and that. Blessings, however, were soon to fall on my three sisters, too, who all managed to rearrange lives and turn up for crucial weeks in June Elgiva, the eldest, remaining for a month—a long time to be away from her husband and home in North Carolina.

Before they arrived, book time was upon us. With surprising ease the first few volumes slipped off to the rare book shop of Jeff Thomas. I decided to start at the top and so chose Jeff, the preeminent rare book expert in the city, a personal acquaintance, and a gem of a man. He arrived on his moped, unfolded his considerable length, removed his helmet, and gasped at the sight that met his eager eyes. Nothing could have prepared him. Every room was lined

with bookcases, many stacked one on top of another. Since the fi-
asco of her book- and book-case-strewn apartment after the '89
earthquake (luckily for her, she was in Boston at the time; unluckily
for me, I was on hand), all the shelves had been bolted to the walls.
However, time and unbridled new interests had expanded her collection and by now every bookcase and large areas of floor in her bedroom and study, even living room sofas, were piled high with
overflow volumes.

"Come in and sit down, if you can clear a space," had become
her usual welcome.

Jeff spent the morning going from shelf to shelf, marking books
that interested him. I looked in on him occasionally, hoping that by
some miracle he would pull out the book that hid the jewelry she
had always kept concealed on a special shelf behind a particular
book.

As I sorted through the piles of books scattered across the floor
after the earthquake, I had stumbled upon a diamond brooch, a diamond watch, and a diamond ring, pieces she sometimes liked to
wear and thus didn't want to keep in the bank, but ones she didn't
want to pay high insurance premiums for. She had rehidden them,
but a year ago when she went to retrieve them for our daughter
Susannah's wedding, she couldn't remember which books marked
their hiding place. My brother-in-law Stephen and I had each
searched shelf after shelf to no avail. Now at last every book was going to be moved. The jewels would be her reward.

Jeff rejoined the two of us going head to head over the piles of
what to any normal mortal would be junk mail covering the dining
room table. This was not a new problem. She and I had been arguing
for years over old editions of *Health* magazine, *Readers Digest* sweep-
stakes, every other mail-order scam known, bank statements, and the
endlessly reshuffled piles of bills and correspondence. It was a rare day
when I could persuade her to clear off the table and return it to its
normal function. Her study desk had long since disappeared from
view, swallowed up by papers, surrounded by the exfoliating library.

Jeff twitched with delight and good humor. "Such an incredibly *intelligent* library," he began. My mother beamed. He'd uttered her favorite word of approbation. "Frankly, I'd like to take every book home with me, but that would not be allowed," he laughed, referring, I assumed, to his wife.

He was curious about the broad range of subjects, the scope of academic interests, the depth of coverage for the elderly widow of a British admiral, raised, for heaven's sake, in Minneapolis. In the library, one of the apartment's three bedrooms, which she had requisitioned for books, from floor to ceiling, corner to corner stretched the classics—Greece, Rome, Egypt—other ancient civilizations, prehistoric cultures, the Celts, Icelandic sagas, the development of language, some European histories, the works of Winston Churchill, her Russian collection, this interest dating from the years before her marriage when she lived with her ambassador uncle as his hostess in Latvia and met so many Russian emigrés. Fine hardcovers, paperbacks, bound journal articles—out into the narrow hallway the piles ran, up through the shelves on China, many volumes going back to the mid-thirties when she went with my father to China for a year, and the spill-over of her interests in Asia—Japan, Southeast Asia, the whole Indian sub-continent, and Tibet. Although she had given a number of volumes on ancient Greece to the Classics Department at San Francisco State, that section of her library was still solid, shelf after shelf attesting to an interest first ignited in the thirties when she spent time in London. For several years during the war when we were living isolated in Scotland, I remember her palpable excitement each time another volume of *The Palace of Minos at Knossos* would arrive, its blue binding and gold lettering representing something quite magical in those drab times. Could she have imagined then that thirty years later she would be living in Athens for her "junior year abroad" as a college student? Or that she'd earn a B.A. and M.A. after she was seventy?

The fabled Silk Route led into the Middle East, with Turkey and the Ottomans arranged side by side with Iran and cultures of the Arab Islamic world, the latter less of an enthusiasm given the subjugation of women. My mother has traveled the globe for over seventy years and spent time in most of the regions that interest her. India, Iran, Turkey, in addition to Greece—she's been to them all more than once and has rugs as well as books and prints to remind her. But she still can't look at her books on the Silk Road and Tibet without sighing her disappointment. "I suppose I'll never travel the Silk Road or reach Tibet now. How I've *longed* to see the monuments of Central Asia. Oh well, let's move ahead with another shelf."

In her bedroom, with just enough space reserved for double bed, dressing table, and chest, lie fiction, biography, miscellaneous treasures. Virginia Woolf, Thomas Mann, Hesse, the Sitwells, Hawthorne, Kafka (her darling Kafka), Faulkner—her taste has been broad and intense. Health, mostly alternative, meditation, diets, herbs, exercise, Jungian psychology, religions (also mostly alternative), self-improvement—the exotic fads of many stripes that have occupied her in waxing and waning waves of enthusiasm. Popular culture, though much derided today, caught her imagination at times too. In the late sixties, she took an extension course on popular music. Books on the Beatles and Rolling Stones sit beside shelves of drama, classic to contemporary, and more than one shelf covering "film" and simply movies—analyses, biographies, guides. The faces of Katherine Hepburn, Elizabeth Taylor, Rudolph Valentino, Lawrence Olivier, and many more smile at the world. She had taken courses on film, too. And of great importance, the world of dance, particularly classical ballet, shows up in book after book—picture books, biographies, histories. She has never forgotten the world of Diaghilev and Nijinsky in prewar Europe and the Royal Ballet of Margo Fonteyn and Nureyev. Stacked all around her bed, under chairs and dressing table lie miscellaneous piles, wondering whether they are headed for her reading list, a space on a shelf, or delivery to a used-book shop or donation center. A duplicate here and there is not unusual. Most likely they would have lingered on in their half-life forever had not the move suddenly loomed.

The dining room shelves were more recent, holding contemporary books she vows to read soon—fiction and memoir, social and political commentaries, journalism. Many come from remainder tables,

some from the used-book room at San Francisco State where she volunteered once a week. "But they only cost a dollar, how could I resist?" would be her reply to my raised eyebrow as her rooms shrank.

The guest room was crammed with treasures. Volumes on megaliths the world over—her precious "standing stones"—and all the
theories that go with them, comprehensive biographies of her favorite musicians—Beethoven, Mozart, Mahler—and the legends who
performed them. American history, an interest that developed the
semester she took the required course in American history while at
San Francisco State for her B.A. degree in Classics. English country
houses, annals of the British navy (we put these aside to be divided
among her grandsons), and leatherbound stud books from my
father's family's racing days. And covering shelf after shelf, her remarkable collection of art history.

At nineteen, living in Latvia with her ambassador uncle, she had
wanted to study art history in Paris. Uncle and father in Minneapolis concurred that such an adventure was out of the question. Some
years later, she had taken an occasional class at the Courtauld Institute in London and started on the long and very circuitous route
that led to a job at the National Gallery of Art in Washington in her
fifties and the B.A. and M.A. in classics after retirement.

Jeff was fascinated and eager to have a few volumes from her collection. Having always bought books because of her interests, not
for their value, she didn't have many of distinct rare-book quality
and luckily was pleased to sell all he chose except for a huge work on
megaliths—"Oh, I can't possibly give that one up"—and a first edi-
tion of T.E. Lawrence's *The Seven Pillars of Wisdom*. Jeff was enor-
mously helpful, suggesting I contact both Moe's and Turtle Island in
Berkeley. There would be plenty of books for both of them. No
problem about competing interests. He'd left any number of tanta-
lizing books to lure them in. Perhaps one of them would be interested in buying everything. That would simplify my life.

But it wasn't to be simple. Family members and friends came in
turn to choose. I'd kept them off until Jeff had made his selections.
My sisters began to arrive in shifts and the selection process started

in earnest. After absurd mathematical calculations involving amount of wall space in the new apartment, number of bookshelves that would fit into said space, and number of books per shelf, we arrived at a total of 1,400 books to go to North Carolina. The library still stood at close to 5,000. Time was shrinking. Where to begin?

It simply had to be *book by book*. First, to make exit passage from the guest room for a large chest I'd sold to an antique dealer, I had to rush through two bookcases of art history. We were batting a little less than fifty–fifty at the end of that session, not quite the ratio needed for 1,400 out of 5,000. The youngest sister, Alexandra, energized as we all were by discovering wonderful treasures in the boxes of silver, is given to multiple allergies and soon found it impossible to sit beside our mother midst the dust of old books. On the second day, Deirdre, usually the one with the most equitable disposition, lost patience and while my mother dozed in the afternoon, simply did her own division of the American history section, our mother none the wiser nor poorer. Deirdre has been a history teacher for many years and knows the wheat from chaff.

June was creeping onward. Deirdre and Alexandra left. Elgiva arrived and we settled down in earnest. Hour upon hour, my own life now on permanent hold, we sat, one or two daughters with their mother, discussing each book in turn.

"Oh, I remember ordering this from Blackwell's, was it 1936 or '37? What a marvelous shop, such service. I know, I need to give up some of these, but the whole question of early man is so fascinating. I need to read this entire collection again. No, I don't want that. I just have no interest in anything French. Well, Madame de Stael. She's a special case. I'd better keep that one. Okay, let's take out that section on poetry. I seldom read poetry nowadays. No, no, keep the T.S. Eliot. I remember when he first read 'The Waste Land' on the radio. I must have Rilke too. We'll soon be coming to Rome. There we can begin to prune. Of course not. We can't sell Gibbon's *Decline and Fall*. You know that was where Wolfgang began trying to educate my sister Priscilla. Perhaps I need to know more about Rome. I'll have plenty of time where I'm going. Ah this one, such an *inter-*

esting book. I can't part with anything on Homer. You know he has been my passion, the reason for learning ancient Greek in the first place."

I turned from silent sighs to vocal reminders. "But *interesting* can't be the criterion. Each book in this apartment is, in some measure, *interesting* to you. That's why you have it. We have to make some discriminations. Which are the most transcendentally *interesting*?" We were all beginning to tire, nerves growing edgy. I was, as usual, talking too much, fearful that the process was taking too long, that she'd still have far too many books left when D-Day arrived.

A long-planned trip to Ashland intervened, providing a few day's respite from the endless sorting. En route, my husband Gray and I, my mother, and Elgiva stopped for coffee. As we were about to leave, my mother, sitting beside me in the booth, announced somewhat petulantly that "*You* won't let me take any books with me." Elgiva was sitting across from her. I asked her who "you" was. "Why, you," was her response.

"What do you mean, me?" I responded. "We have all been in this together."

"Well, it's you who's making all these decisions; they are kinder than you," was her reply.

I froze. Pent up frustration and rage seethed. I felt like an unfairly used child. For the rest of the trip (four hours) I chose silence, not trusting what I would say. My mother tried to apologize, it was only a joke, but it was too late.

A few days in the Ashland sun thawed the frost a little, but I announced to Elgiva that she was on her own with the books from then on. The look of terror on her face was daunting. By the time we returned to San Francisco, I had relented, but each day was doubly taxing—trying to hold my tongue as Ruth studied the title page, discussed the circumstances of book after book. Dustjacket praise proved endlessly validating to her. Deadlines for a final sale before moving day were growing closer; the number of books to be handled refused to diminish fast enough. We kept forging ahead, Elgiva and I slipping a volume here and there back onto the shelf for the dealers to come instead of into the bags and boxes for the movers. We had to control the numbers.

Elgiva and I survived on laughs, sometimes late in the evening. One night after ten we were pushing shopping carts across the parking lot behind the apartment, taking away yet more boxes of debris under cover of darkness to a bin we had discovered. I looked at her and asked, "What are we doing, two dignified sisters over sixty, two old ladies, pushing around grocery wagons piled with trash?" In those chaotic yet focused weeks we grew close in ways we had never thought possible in our closest moments heretofore, and swore we'd start throwing out most of our possessions. We couldn't will such a legacy to our own children.

It had to happen. We finished the selecting process. The numbers were close enough—about 1,500 books would go with her to fit, we hoped, into the fifteen bookcases allotted. I began to find sympathy in my heart for a plucky lady who had stayed independent so long, who had made a new life for herself each time something of one life had been taken, who was determined from a young age to find a place for the intellectual that was part of her, whose interests were constantly expanding. She had one husband, five children, fourteen grandchildren, fourteen great-grandchildren and counting, a universe of friends…and *her books*. Ruth's books were like children to her, extensions of herself, reflecting the fabric of her life. She was ready to move on. But this severance was a partial death, evoking memories from every corner of a complex life. Could we blame her for exhaustion and sorrow? She hardly blinked as we sorted through the photos, letters, and diaries. It was her library that held her in thrall and for which she was beginning to mourn.

The final-stage book dealers were interesting and also competitive. Jeff was wrong in thinking that I could easily deal with two people at once. But eventually every book found its way out the door, the final selections going in eighty boxes to a hard-working young man with a new shop on Irving Street and twenty empty bookcases to a used-furniture store. No diamonds had shown up, so we called the insurance company. She could realize only a small sum without the extra schedule. "No, she couldn't have lost them because they had never left the apartment. Yes, they could have been stolen—a maid, a maintenance man, no, we had no one in particular."

Her friends Len and Beverly Coleman dropped by the Sunday before she left. They were collecting the cookbooks she'd given them and while there, looking through the remaining kitchen debris before I packed it up for the Good Will. I'd offered an excellent collection of kitchen items to a furniture/junk dealer, but he had turned up his nose at the dishes and pots and pans. Her maid Jane had taken several items and so had I. Not much was left. Len emerged from the kitchen, shaking a plastic container he'd pulled from the far reaches of a corner cupboard.

"I think Ruth may want these," he said lightly. I opened the lid. Inside lay three jewelry boxes. "Guess she hid them so well, no one was ever going to find them," he laughed. Ruth could summon no memory of when or why they had been concealed in such an odd place. We were all beginning to look like characters in an O. Henry story. She felt a little foolish when she called her insurance agent. I speculated on the behavior of the final furniture dealer and/or the Good Will representative had they been the ones to open the box.

The jewelry lies secure in a North Carolina safety deposit box. Ruth has defied all odds and is blissfully satisfied with her new life in a state she always said she was happy to leave in 1956 after ten mid-life years there. The walls of her apartment are lined with enough reading to carry her into her 125th year.

JEAN GANSA

Trying to Get Ready

THE LAST TIME I TOOK MY FATHER in for a medical check up, his physician took an especially long time listening to my father's heart. I noticed but I didn't notice.

I said, which I usually don't, "He is doing very well."

To which the doctor replied, "Well, you never can tell with someone his age," which is something the doctor usually doesn't say.

My father, Allan Charles, is ninety-two years old now. He has had a very full and successful life as a lawyer, community board member, athlete, amateur carpenter, husband, and father. All he has left of these activities and roles is father. His hearing, sight, and mind aren't what they used to be. You can tell because I am tempted to talk to the doctor about him when he is right there—as though he isn't a full participant in the decisions about his life right now.

My father's father died when he was a young boy of six and he grew up in a household of women—his grandmother, mother, and sister. After the death of his father, his mother studied for the Bar and became the first woman Justice of the Peace in Santa Clara county. My father's grandmother was principal of a local girl's school. They both, his grandmother (as an adult) and his mother, had graduated from Stanford. The family had been invited to come to Palo Alto by Senator Stanford to attend his new university—as had his father's family.

After being a track star at Stanford, then a law school graduate, he married my mother and had two daughters. So you can see that my father has been accustomed to living with women, and pretty bossy ones at that. He was and still is handsome, courtly, and charming to women. One of his law partners said that you could never get behind him in an elevator and I remember my friend Georgina telling me that her mother had said she was sorry for my father because he would always be surrounded by women at cocktail parties. I never had the feeling that my father saw that as a problem.

My father was a trial lawyer. Someone told me one of the reasons he was so successful was that, besides doing a lot of research, he was so polite in the courtroom that the opposing lawyers couldn't believe he could win. They lost before they knew what happened. Of course it is hard for me to really know how others saw my father, especially because my sister and I have never gotten over adoring him. We both still call him Daddy. It is sort of embarrassing, especially when we go out with him and find a waiter, usually from a foreign country, who, after hearing my sister or me call him Daddy, starts to call him Daddy too.

My father played tennis well into his eighties and continued to go to his office even though he could no longer practice law. His firm kept an office for him until he was ninety-two. In honor of his ninetieth birthday, the firm had a portrait painted of him. My sister and I unveiled it and both immediately hated it. He looked like a tough old man. Everything in his face went downhill. His eyes drooped, his mouth went down on the edges, and the wrinkles in his forehead made him look like he was scowling. It may have been just right for a tough old trial lawyer and to scare summer law students who would study in the Charles Room, but it certainly didn't please us. To me he is still handsome with very blue eyes, a warm smile, and a kindly look. Is he really that tough to some people? I was sure that could not be true, until recently.

After my mother's death at the age of seventy-four in 1971, I started taking my father to church with me. As a child, my father occasionally attended the Unitarian Church, but church was never part of my family life growing up. For the sake of being with me, he came and still does. He even accompanies my husband and me up to the altar for communion, but he cannot imagine why anyone would eat those tasteless wafers dipped in horrible-tasting wine. He will put the wafer in his mouth, but he will not swallow it, much to the dismay of the servers and my husband. I am somewhat embarrassed as he walks down the aisle with it sticking out of his mouth until we sit down and I pull out a Kleenex and wrap the wafer in it, but I can understand his position. I told our rector that my father had been raised as a Unitarian and that that is why he won't swallow the wafer. At a party recently the rector told me that a visiting cleric asked him, "Who is that old man who is fixing his beady eye on the wafer?" When he told me that, I was shocked and then had to realize that I have a very special vision of my father that makes me blind to how some others might see him.

Sometimes I feel as if I speak for my father too much. It is hard to tell how tuned in he is. He is inclined to start saying something that doesn't end up making sense. On the other hand, the other day the wife of a close friend whom he hasn't seen for years died and I asked my father if he would like to call him. My father replied that he thought he ought to. He cannot dial a phone and I was worried about how he might be with his friend, but I made the call and when I turned the phone over to my father, he told his friend that we sent our sympathy to him and his conversation was quite appropriate. It made me wonder again if I were stepping in and taking over too much.

There are times when he butters his butter, can't remember that he has just eaten and asks me where Jean is (my name is Jean). He definitely cannot find his way home anymore. When he walks uphill he has to move very slowly; he is somewhat bent over and looks his age. He has had pneumonia at least twice and been in intensive care. The other day when I was taking him to the dermatologist for a

check-up, he suddenly started shaking all over and couldn't stop. Fortunately, he was in the doctor's office. The doctor checked his heart
and said to just take him home right away. It turned out that he was
coming down with an infection and once we got a hold of the internist and put him on an antibiotic, he was back to normal in one day.

I could tell stories about my father over and over with great feeling and delight. When we were back east visiting an old friend of
my husband's who had just recently remarried at seventy, I told
about something my father had just done. Our friend's new wife said
with the lift of an eyebrow and the lowering of the sides of her
mouth, "Oh, more father stories." Was I being boring? Was she
feeling a little too close to my father's age for comfort? She was seventy-five at the time.

At any rate, getting back to my struggle for preparedness for my
father's dying, I do understand that I will never be totally ready and
that I cannot prevent the shock and feelings of deep sadness and
who knows what at the time of his death. I did have a dream several
years ago of my father walking into the surf and not being able to
get him before he disappeared. I awoke with a feeling of great sadness that stayed with me all day. Some part of me has been prepar-
ing. However, I have this feeling that I have much stronger feelings
than I can acknowledge. For example, my husband one day started
the car before my father was totally in, and I yelled at him to stop
the car which he did immediately. What scared me was how furious
I was at my husband and how unforgiving I sensed I would be if my
father had really been hurt. It was the same feeling I would have toward someone who might hurt one of my children. I have a feeling
of foreboding that my feelings of sadness and grief will be more
powerful than anything I have dealt with so far.

Somewhere in here I need to add that if I had the full-time responsibility of caring for my father, I'd go nuts. So I need to thank
my father for having been able to save enough money in his life that
he can afford to live the way he does.

My mother died five long years after she had had a debilitating
stroke. She could barely talk because her mouth and throat were

partially paralyzed. Her incredible wisdom, energy, and intelligence were no longer available to her. She had to go back into the hospital for surgery on a blood clot in her brain and did not want to live. The specialists were determined to save her even when her family and internist said to let her go. Only when her pneumonia returned for the third time in her last hospital visit did they finally give up and let her go. I knew she would be better off.

I don't have that same feeling about my father. He still lives in his old familiar home, he has life around him—a grandson with his wife and baby live with him and he seems happy and he is always glad to see me and my sister. He employs two women who are sisters and had helped with my mother. They trade off taking care of him and are both very fond of him and he of them.

So does he have to get to a place of being really miserable most of the time for me to be ready for him to die? I know I would wish for him that he would just die in his sleep when the time is right for him. It seems like these days that doesn't happen for many people I know. Some of what I have found hard has been going through the illnesses he has had. Will he die this time? I remember once quite a few years ago when I took him to the emergency room on a weekend and he told me that each time that happens he wonders whether this is it. I don't think he could verbalize that now.

Just writing this helps me feel more peaceful, at least right now. My husband reminded me after he read what I had written that it is really an enjoyable part of my life to pick him up and go out to the tennis club for lunch once a week or to take him to church. I will really miss that. There will be a big empty space in my life when he dies.

MARY THACHER

An Unexpected Pleasure

I WAS PACKING MY SUITCASE in early June, feeling very despondent. Why had I decided to take this trip? I could have been going up to the country to our haven in the sun. Of course, a few days in New York are always a treat, but that was not the main purpose of the trip. No, I had opted to go to my 45th Vassar Reunion, Class of '49, in Poughkeepsie, New York. Though I had been in the East many times, I had never been tempted to return to the campus in all those intervening years. For a year I had been barraged with mail from Vassar telling me how wonderful the reunion would be. I briefly weighed the pros and cons and decided against going. Then I began to get adorable messages from classmates I had never known, asking me to summarize my life for the past forty-five years. The mere thought had me in a panic—even more so after I heard the awesome, impressive, and amusing summary one of my friends had written for her Stanford reunion. Over the years I had received annual postcards from the alumni asking me to report on my activities and had never returned one, so why would I start now? The point was that I was at Vassar for two years and had made only five friends, and two of them had already passed away. Even my roommate and I had lost track of each other once she married a young German immigrant and moved to Nova Scotia.

I had been giving money to Vassar all those years because I genuinely believed that it had offered me a superior education. But it was also true that I had not even liked it there. I had attended a Sacred Heart convent for six years. I was seventeen and incredibly young and naive for my years. At the convent I had been a big fish in a very little pond. I had been President of the student body but just about everyone I met those first days at Vassar had also been President of the student body, but in schools with hundreds of students. All that eastern sophistication threw me. I had always been a friendly person and would go up and speak to almost anyone. That was not the eastern way. They would ask where I was from and when I said, "San Francisco," their only comment would be "Have you been to Hollywood?" I had not even been to Los Angeles, let alone the East. The Second World War had just ended and most of the students had never been west of the Hudson. The servicemen had not yet returned to tell their tales of California. I became so shy that I would barely speak to anyone. I often wouldn't go to dinner because as I would look around for a table at which to sit, napkins would be put on the backs of chairs and the girls would say, "These are saved."

On the other hand, I genuinely like the current president, an attractive, dynamic young Wellesley graduate whom I had met on several occasions in San Francisco. I recently had been persuaded to go to an alumni evening at which slides were shown of their new art museum, The Frances Lehmann Loeb, designed by Caesar Pelli. It was both innovative and classic and I knew that I would enjoy seeing it. Vassar has also acquired some fine works of art during its hundred and twenty-five years of existence.

It had never occurred to me to ask Carter, my husband, to come with me, so sure was I that he would resist. Then one morning I awoke very early and began thinking about the reunion. I had an inspiration. Carter likes to sleep a little later on the weekends. Even so, I prodded Carter, I hope gently, until I knew that he was somewhat awake. I said, "You must come to the Vassar 45th Reunion with me."

"Why would I want to do that?" he queried.

"Because you always make me go to your Yale Law School reunions!"

There was a groan, and then he said, "If you'll just let me go back to sleep, *I'll go!*" I couldn't believe it. I jumped out of bed, elated. When Carter emerged for breakfast—and I did fix him an especially good one—he likewise could not believe what he had said. But he didn't renege. He allowed as how he had never been to Vassar and he wouldn't mind seeing it.

As the time drew nearer, he grumbled more frequently. "It's not a convenient time, I will just have returned from New Jersey from a meeting I must attend, I'd rather be moving up to Napa for the summer," and on and on. Even I began to have grave misgivings.

The June weather in New York was superb, clear and sunny, but not too hot. We rushed around trying to absorb all that available culture. We walked miles within the Metropolitan Museum and saw a fascinating exhibit of pre-Impressionist paintings, the newly opened Chinese Garden, and remodeled Sculpture Garden on the roof.

Then came Friday, the afternoon on which we were to appear at Vassar. We drove to Poughkeepsie with another couple, one of the three living classmates I had known. The incredible spring green of the enormous deciduous trees such as maples, beeches, and eastern oaks, as well as the lovely views of the Hudson River, were a joy to see. An impressive stone archway announced the main entrance to the college. To the right of the gate was the largest ginkgo tree I have ever seen. Matthew Vassar surely must have planted it when he founded the college in 1861. He was a Poughkeepsie businessman and philanthropist. I knew the thousand-acre campus was beautiful but I had not remembered how truly magnificent the grounds were. The earliest buildings consisted of Main, a large cumbersome edifice where all the seniors were housed, and then four red-brick buildings, four stories each, which formed the quad, which made a harmonious central area. Carter looked properly impressed. We finally found the house where the Class of '49 was assigned. It was clearly one of the oldest and most in need of remodeling, which I am sure the college wanted to impress upon us. We were assigned a sparse room with two cots and two desks over which two bulbs hung from cords in the ceiling, reminiscent of a stark Francis Bacon painting. The bathroom for our half of the corridor, serving about twelve rooms, was at the end of the hall and consisted of one shower, one bathtub, two sinks, and two johns. I noted that Carter looked horrified at the prospect of sharing the bathroom with the ladies.

It was a glorious summer evening and a delicious dinner was served, catered by the Culinary Institute of America, headquartered in Poughkeepsie, and held on an expansive green lawn, the type you rarely see in the West. Right away we saw the Morrisons, the only couple we knew, which cheered Carter immensely. George and Carter had been classmates at Yale Law School and his wife Lucy and I had been freshmen in the same house. But she hadn't been a friend. In fact, I don't think she ever spoke to me. I can remember meeting Lucy. She epitomized my ideal of the All-American beauty. She was very tall with dark, wavy shoulder-length, shiny brown hair. A perfect set of teeth radiated from her tanned face, and with her lovely smile, she was the exact image of a Vogue debutante. By contrast, I was very short and had nondescript brown hair. To make matters worse, we had to attend an exercise class once a week. Lucy and I were in the same class. The first day, Miss Tims said to us, "Now I will show you three different physical types. There is the Short and Stocky. Miss Wilbur, will you please come to the center of the room." I could barely keep from crying as I went to the center in my leotard. Then she picked someone to exemplify the Medium build, and needless to say, she chose Lucy for the Tall and Lean.

Lucy wore blue jeans to classes during the week. It is hard to imagine today but that was the first time I had ever seen blue jeans worn in school, or even pants of any kind. I was from the West but I thought only cowboys wore jeans. My wardrobe consisted of wool skirts, blouses, Sloppy Joe baggy sweaters, and brown and white saddle shoes. Lucy belonged to the avant guard, very wealthy New

York group, of which there seemed to be a goodly number in our dorm. Then on Fridays, Lucy would don the most sophisticated clothes I had ever seen—glamorous, low-cut dresses and to complete the picture, a full-length fur coat. She and her friends would rush off in cabs to the train station headed for New York to a debut party. I was mesmerized. I also was to be a "deb" in San Francisco at Christmas, but I would never have admitted it as I thought it was a phony social custom.

Now, seeing her after all these years, I looked at her anew and I was no longer in awe. George, her husband, was tall and still good-looking, but as with all of us, the years showed. He looked a bit paunchy and self-satisfied. Lucy still had a perfect figure, wore an expensive "just right" print dress, and Ferragamo shoes with low heels. In fact, Carter remarked later that they both looked a little pale and joyless. George had retired from a prestigious law firm started by his wife's father. He is a Trustee of Yale Law School. They live in New York City, and have a hundred-year-old farmhouse in New Jersey, inherited from her family, and a home on the Portuguese coast. "And do you have children?" "Yes, one son," Lucy replied, "and he sells religious books in New York City." She did not seem to want to dwell on him, so I thought it might be a store selling books on the Moonies or another such group. I found out later that it was a well-respected Episcopalian bookstore.

Before leaving for the East, I had my hair cut, colored, and curled. I remember making the conjecture that three quarters of the class would probably have gray, short hair that required no beauty salon but only a shower and hair dryer to make them look ready for a party. I was about right. Lucy was among the one quarter like me, except that I couldn't help noticing that her hair did look quite thin. I suspected that she had had a facelift.

Saturday night Carter asked me to stand guard outside the bathroom while he brushed his teeth and I replied, "How ridiculous!" and he did manage to accomplish it without interruption. The next morning, Carter, not an early riser, woke me at five-thirty A.M. and announced that he was determined to have his shower without any ladies nearby. Of course, he never travels with a bathrobe, so he carefully bundled up his clothes and took them with him. He returned, immensely relieved to have been solo. As it was still so early, we decided to take a walk on that crisp, beautiful morning. We ended up in a cemetery. There is something endlessly fascinating about old New England cemeteries. Often they are studded with vintage trees with gnarled trunks and dead limbs. The trees were there but obviously this had not been a cemetery for the rich, because the gray, granite markers were not large or impressive. They seemed to date mostly from the early part of the nineteenth century. Many of them were wildly askew. A few had those terrible bunches of plastic flowers. I imagine that many of the descendants had moved to other parts of the country. It had a desolate, uncared-for appearance. After a welcome cup of coffee with the local taxi driver and newspaper deliverer at the only café open, we returned to campus.

The high point of the weekend was the walk from the center of campus, the quad, by classes, up a hill to the gym where box lunches were to be served and the various classes honored. Each class carried different-colored balloons. The band played lively music, and it was the moment when you had a genuine feeling of shared experiences. Carter couldn't get over the Class of 1929. They arrived in convertibles. About a dozen of these stalwarts, in their mid-nineties, mounted the stairs alone onto the dais, amidst huge cheers. Large banners announced the amounts donated by each reunion class and they were impressive. It was exciting to see the large numbers of the younger classes there with their spouses and young children. They looked so fresh, lively, and filled with vitality. It made me feel that Vassar still had an important role to play in present day education.

Dinner that evening was held in the house where we were staying with out own classmates. There were many more women than men. I didn't know the people we sat with but they were an interesting group. I was particularly impressed with how the "single" women had worked out their lives, single because of being widowed, divorced, or never married. Many had taken up careers later in life and were doing everything from working in bookstores to innovating needed social service programs in their communities.

That night in the bathroom while brushing our teeth together, I met the couple across the hall from us. I admired her "just right" travel bathrobe—neat, lightweight and yet warm enough. I had noticed her very tall, rather frail-looking husband, who had the appearance of wishing he were some place other than Vassar. The next morning, sure enough, I saw the same woman in the bathroom. Joan looked at me quizzically and said, "My, you have a persistent husband." I knew right away that something was up and a tale was about to be unfolded. It seems that about five in the morning, after going to the bathroom, Carter had taken a left instead of a right turn and had wandered into their room across the hall from us. He tried to get into Joan's bed and she pushed him away. But in his half-sleep he was not to be deterred and tried again. Finally her annoyed husband said, "Just get him out of here!" At this point I guess Joan firmly ushered him to the door and into our room. I was blissfully unaware of the drama and didn't even wake up.

We had planned to have breakfast and then go to the train station. But after recounting this tale, Carter said, "We ought to take an earlier train into New York." I pleaded for breakfast, but Carter assured me that we could get something to eat or drink at the station. I don't think he was going to take the chance of meeting up with Joan and her husband. By this time it was pouring rain and cold. We got to the station way too early and, needless to say, there was not even a hot drink vending machine of any kind. It was a long chilly return trip to New York.

Was I glad that I had gone to the reunion? For me, it was not really a reunion, as I had known so few people. Rather it was a reviewing after forty-five years. I came away genuinely impressed with the vitality and integrity of the administration and the students. The addition of men seemed a great improvement. There are now almost an equal number of men, and they are a talented group. It is still a great privilege to attend small classes taught by professors who truly care. Vassar continues to be very innovative in allowing students to plan their own majors.

I was particularly pleased that Carter had thoroughly enjoyed his first visit to Vassar. We were both impressed with the new Art Museum and I have kept an active interest in it since the reunion. Yes, I was definitely glad that I had attended. I only regretted that if I had not been so immature as a student, I would have been able to take greater advantage of the opportunities that were offered.

JOANN REINHARDT

The Reunion

A TURKISH FOLK TALE
*Little Ahmet is going to be hanged. The Imam comes to him and
says, "Ahmet, thank Allah." Ahmet says, "Why should I thank
Allah? I'm going to be hanged."*

*Then an edict comes down from the Sultan. Ahmet is to be
skinned alive and then hanged.*

"You see?" said the Imam.

I HAD BEEN FEELING A LITTLE sick and lacking in energy,
with the usual tourist complaint for two weeks since coming home
from a trip to Central Asia. I felt I had to begin feeling energetic
again because on Thursday we were expecting my old friend Barbara
and her husband, Terry, to arrive, and with my husband, Dick, we
were all going off to Stanford that evening for the start of our forty-
fifth reunion weekend. Sensing that I might have some bug that
would show up in a test, I took a specimen to the lab on Thursday
afternoon.

Dinner on the Stanford Quad that night was magical. The air
was soft and warm and the candles on the tables cast a glowing light
on everything and everybody. Could it possibly have been forty-five
years? We all looked pretty good in that glamorous setting.

Dinner looked delicious and everyone else ate heartily. I thought
it tasted like straw. The main course seemed to be duck, and was
that rice or couscous, or what? The only things that tasted good
were the wine and salad and roll. I tasted a little dessert too, but was
content to leave most of it. Could I possibly be turning into the kind
of person who could take food or leave it, who could take one taste

of dessert and leave the rest, satisfied by that one taste? What a happy thought.

Friday's events started with a box lunch. Why do they put so much food into those boxes? People throw most of it away. I ate a tiny piece of my roll and some white meat of chicken, and put my wrapped chocolate brownie into my purse, in case I wasn't turning into the kind of person who doesn't care about dessert.

We then went to afternoon classes. I staked out "ladies rooms" all along the way, noticing that bathrooms and drinking fountains at Stanford have vastly improved in forty-five years.

I was beginning to feel very ragged and called my doctor to see if my test results were in. They were. The nurse said I had giardia and two other intestinal parasites. She said I must get to a pharmacy immediately so a prescription could be called in.

The pharmacist came down personally from his elevated command post to tell me that I must not have one drop of alcohol with the medication, Flagyl, or I would have a violent reaction. Also, I must stay off all dairy products, salads, and fats.

"Sorry about that," he said, gazing at my reunion badge.

The big event of the weekend was that night, Friday, when our class was having its dinner dance. Barbara and Terry went from our Palo Alto motel to the party by cab so I could nap for an hour. When Dick and I finally arrived, the cocktail hour was over and people were getting seated. An old friend rushed up and said she was holding a place for us at their table. As it turned out, every woman at the table was wearing a red dress. It was like a table of aged Stanford Dollies without the pompons!

Evidently the word had spread quickly during cocktails that I had a roaring case of giardia. It turned out during the evening that just about everyone at the party also seemed to have had giardia—last month, last year, twice last year, or their sister or even their dog had just gotten over it.

"You know, you can't have a drop of alcohol," they said, cheerfully, sipping their chardonnay.

I was feeling pretty terrible but knew I looked all right since I had a little fever and my cheeks were pink and my eyes a little too bright. No one seemed to notice, anyway, because after the searching look and a "how are you *feeling*?" giardia stories began to unfold.

"Listen, when we were in Nepal...."

"...and we were hiking in the Sierras when the dog got sick...."

"...so my doctor didn't even wait for the test but put me right on Flagyl...."

"...and I just got over giardia and got some parasite from meat!"

I don't recall a single conversation about grandchildren or retirement or about how they should bring back the Stanford Indian or Western Civ.

So thank you, Allah, for sending me giardia at my forty-fifth reunion. You could have sent it on the fourteen-hour drive from Urgench to Merv, or on the ten-hour flight home from London to San Francisco. Instead, you made me the conversational hit of the party.

AVA JEAN BRUMBAUM

Getting On

IGNORE IT THOUGH I WOULD LIKE TO, I am being forced to notice that my friends, as my mother used to say, are "getting on." And so it follows and must be true that I, too, am "getting on." But my mind does not readily accept the hints that my body keeps on sending.

There are such reminders, of course. When I go on a trip, my clothes and cosmetics are still manageable; it's only my medicine kit that takes so long to pack and is so heavy to tote around. And my tennis foursome, which has played regularly once a week for thirty-six years, now seldom has four members who are up to playing all at once. Our get-togethers these days are often just luncheon parties and include a lot of show-and-tell about our various ailments—or "organ recitals," as one friend calls them.

So much time is required each day just for routine body maintenance that if you do it all there's little time left for anything else. There are range-of-motion and stretching exercises, aerobic walking and Kegel drills, and the naps and hot tubs to soothe aching joints after gardening or tennis. Lay off for a week or two, and it all falls apart and you're back to square one.

And those bodily reminders of mine grow ever more plentiful: diverticulitis, arthritis, blepheritis, hay fever, Sjogren's disorder, hiatus hernia, Reynaud's disease, a tummy that lives on Tums, to name but a few. When I paid a visit to a new doctor recently, husband Harold said, "Just tell him about the Top Ten."

To start from the bottom up, there are my feet. My arches had forever been a problem. Then a hammer toe started to stick up and rub against my shoe so badly that a podiatrist sold me an amazing contraption: an iron ball with a ring fitting over it on two sides of long-handled tongs. With the proper solution put on the shoe and this apparatus screwed into place, a bump would appear on my shoe which made room for my poor toe. When, after a couple of years, this remedy ceased to work, my orthopedist-brother cut off the offending joint, leaving me with a floppy toe, but after a while I could wear dress shoes again. The podiatrist also suggested Birkenstocks. Though awfully Berkeley and ugly, those sandals were delightfully comfortable, and I found myself wearing them around the house—though I wouldn't be caught dead in public with them on. But after a few years of this my city shoes began to hurt again, and I found that although, when young, I had worn a AA width, now I needed a C—if I could find one. For a second time, all my old shoes had to be given away, and for me, now, it's only low-heeled, round-toed "menopause Mary Janes."

Next came my eyes. A small detached retina required surgery and a week of lying semi-recumbent with my head to one side. Then there followed surgery to take tucks in the eyelids that were encroaching on my vision. Three cheers, then, for Medicare: the only silver lining in those clouds. But doctors can't do everything, and in desperation over all the bodily complaints they couldn't fix, I turned to alternative forms of treatment. So now acupuncture, Chinese herbs, massage therapy, and yoga have been added to my list of remedies and, I think, are helping certain things, though I can't be sure.

Then came the Accidents. First, I was knocked flat onto our barn's concrete floor while foolishly feeding carrots to four eager horses at once who didn't have the manners to take turns. Luckily, I didn't get trampled in the scuffle, but, no longer healing quickly, my shoulder hurt for a long time. Then, a few months later, while riding full-tilt on a gravel road, I lost my balance and landed hard. It wasn't the horse's fault, but rather, forgetting my age and thinking I could ride an English saddle with no pommel to hang on to, I was just not paying attention to reality.

Having skied all my life and had many spills, why did this year's fall affect me so badly? A hard one on an icy slope injured that shoulder once again, so twice-weekly visits to a physical therapist have been added to my fitness routine. Moreover, on my second visit, I found that the therapist was into "auras," leading Harold to wonder what kooky thing I'd get involved with next.

When you add to this maintenance program the usual check-ups involving mammograms, chest X-rays, pap smears, eye checks, skin cancer checks, sygmoidoscopies, and (now that my gums are receding) more frequent trips to the dentist, there hardly seems time just to live. There must be a message here, and I think it's starting to percolate through. Today I called my skiing buddy of forty years and told her to find another roommate for next year at Alta. As for horses, I love them as pets, but if I ride again it will be at a walking gait and western style. I know I won't climb Mount Tallac at Fallen Leaf Lake again: it's kinder trails for me from now on, and even cross-country trekking is out.

But now for a good soak in the spa and off to bed, with a pillow under one arm, another under my knees, an icebag on my shoulder, a heating pad wherever it's needed at the moment, and a long-suffering husband who can't settle down until I've adjusted all that paraphernalia.

Coda

SUSAN RENFREW

Only Connect

THE MESSAGE MACHINE clicked on. "This is Roger, I've been so worried about you. Hope the operation went well. I never seem to find time to write, but you know how I am. If you have been wondering what I've been up to, the play went well. I have a producer who wants to bring it to the States. Now take care of yourselves and let me know what is happening."

I pressed the save button. Roger? Who is Roger? I didn't recognize the voice. The poor man must have dialed the wrong number. And he's calling from another country to someone who has had an operation, but they will never know he cares. He said "yourselves." For some reason something like this makes me sad thinking of all the lost communications. I remembered letters I had written, one to my grandfather who had a sudden case of pneumonia the week before I was married. After the wedding as we were driving away, my husband said, "We're going to Cleveland tomorrow. Your grandfather died." And then I understood why my parent's door which was never locked was locked for a time on the day before the wedding and why my father had tears in his eyes as he walked me down the aisle.

I found my unopened letter on my grandfather's desk after the funeral, telling him how sorry I was that he was sick. In high school, I wrote a friend's father who had cancer telling him how special he was, but he too died without reading the letter.

A few months after the message from Roger, I was listening to my messages. "Hey, Sinclairs, I'm visiting my mother in Vermont. Her number is 802-243-8967. It's been so long since I've heard from you. Mary broke her arm last month which kept her from her novel. Things are so-so for me. That pain keeps persisting. Call me." I recognized Roger's voice. It didn't sound as if he'd heard from the Sinclairs. My son Rob would say, "Mom you always butt into everyone's business." It's not my business and yet...poor man. His voice has a forced cheerfulness. I could call, but Vermont? That will be expensive.

"Hello, this is Sue Renfrew."

An elderly woman's voice answered. "What? Never heard of you."

"Do you have a son named Roger?"

"That is hardly any of your business." (She must know Rob.)

"I live in San Francisco and...."

"I don't know anyone there." She was irritated now.

"Roger called a couple named Sinclair but had my phone number by mistake."

"I don't know what you are talking about. Roger isn't here."

"Please would you give him a message for me."

"But who are you? I don't know you."

"Please just tell him he is calling the wrong number when he phones the Sinclairs."

"Well, if you know so much, what is their number?"

"I'm sorry, I don't know. I don't know them, I don't know Roger and I don't know you, but I do care that he is told that his messages are not reaching them."

She was quiet for a while. "He goes to England tomorrow. I am lost without him. What did you say your name was? I'll tell him you called."

NANCY GENN

Planes of Light: An Introduction to Our Cover

I AM IN A CREATIVE PERIOD, the work is flowing. When I leave the studio, the images recur as I mentally review details. Why are these works special? I think it is because everything has come together in just the right balance. They are a logical development, a combination of techniques of various media I have used in the past. These monotypes combine painting, printmaking, and the addition of handmade papers. The total shape is influenced by my experience as a sculptor.

Work on these monotypes begins in my studio, not at the press. At first the image is tentative, built up in thin layers of paint. These first transparent layers develop the emerging form, create a richness, set the tone and spirit of the work. Layering of color controls tone and density, but the freshness must be guarded, as it is easy to lose, easy to become labored. I work into the damp paper with pencil, the pencil line a guide, a freehand line seeking possibilities. Gradually the emerging shapes are accentuated and clarified, inviting variation. At this early stage, all is open to exploration.

I like to work in series; a serious idea deserves a thorough development. In the reiterations, atmosphere and a sense of place emerge. My *Planes of Light* series focuses on a diagonal plane intersecting a rectangle. Although the first of these paintings was done in November 1989, while I was a visiting artist at the American Academy in Rome, I'm still working on their successors eight years later, using fine papers from Japan and incorporating the vertical format of intersection planes developed in Rome. On some of these Japanese papers I have etched calligraphic lines.

In 1988 and 1989, I began painting into the paper first, with stains and washes, and using Plexiglass plates to lay down the blocks of color. In the second year I cut the plates to follow the image. The plate parts were inked separately, then resembled and the image pulled. I enjoyed the possibilities for change in each image, allowing a thorough exploration of the idea. I began printing in 1991 at Kala Institute in Berkeley, where space is provided for printmakers to share facilities, large and small presses, and many tools. Since then I have continued to use Plexiglass plates. After printing I bring the monotypes back to my studio for study, further refinement, and final development. Sometimes I paint into them again to push them farther. Every stroke should be anchored. I must fight with each element, a space or a line so that it is really there. At this time I may add layers of etched and other printed papers. Creating an enclosure pulls separate forms together. Adjusting a corner can mean tearing off an inch to push the plane back or to pull it forward to give it a stronger direction to create opposition and tension. This process is like designing a building. The architecture in my work may be hidden, but it is always present.

The calligraphic line that runs across some of the shapes appears in my painting of the late 1950s and 1960s as well as in my linear cast-bronze sculptures of the 1970s. It is a surprise to me to see this calligraphy line return to my work, but this time it is a foil set down on a defined geometric structure, rather than the structure upon which the form is built as in the bronzes.

I've recently begun to travel in Central Asia and the region's many layers of cultures—Christian and Muslim overlaid with archaeological remnants of Greek, Roman, and Lycian civilizations— inspire interesting combinations of images and motifs, and blended signs and symbols. In my series of paintings I want to explore the interplay of light and geometric forms influenced by such calligraphy and architecture. All my life I have been attracted to the sea. It's an important visual and metaphorical source for me, and in my travels along the Turkish coast I have found sources of inspiration such as that reflected in *Marmaris* on our cover.

Ava Jean Barber Brumbaum was born and raised in Berkeley, graduating from U.C. Berkeley with a degree in bacteriology and zoology. After working for two years at the Crocker Radiation Lab, marriage to Harold Pischel "seemed a good option." She moved to San Francisco, raised four children, and considered herself lucky to be able to choose a volunteer career, much of it centered around the symphony—where she holds the track record for board membership, fifty years and still counting. She has also contributed considerable time and energy to the Conservatory of Music and recently served as chaplain's aid on the AIDS ward at San Francisco General Hospital. Widowed and remarried (to her second Harold), she retired nine years ago to rural West Marin, where she keeps busy gardening, playing tennis, entertaining grandchildren, and thoroughly enjoying country life.

Margaret Evans Gault was born in Los Angeles and grew up on the West Side. Following graduation from Vassar College—where, one assumes, she did not take classes in ceramics—she married attorney James Gault, and together they came west to San Francisco. After raising a family of four children (three, not surprisingly, are boys), she became a secondary school teacher, instructing unwed mothers, forbidden in those days from attending public school. On retirement from teaching, she assumed a second professional career as a financial advisor.

Born in San Francisco, **Jean Charles Gansa** is a fourth-generation Stanford graduate. Her grandmother and great grandmother attended Stanford together, allowing the four generations to fit into the one hundred-year life span of the university. As her children grew up, she earned an M.A. in Clinical Psychology at the University of San Francisco. She now has a private practice in psychotherapy and leads seminars through The Guild for Psychological Studies on spiritual and psychological subjects. Her current focus is on finding meaning in old age. She has five children, all in California, two grandchildren, three stepsons, and a step-grandchild. She and second husband Alex enjoy foreign travel, including seeing Alex's relatives in Russia, Latvia, and Germany.

Nancy Thompson Genn is an accomplished artist who has exhibited her work worldwide—New York, Tokyo, London, her native San Francisco. Her work is represented in the Museum of Modern Art in New York and in San Francisco, in the Albright-Knox Museum in Buffalo, the National Museum of Fine Arts in Washington, D.C., the Library of Congress, and a number of additional museums in California. Over the years, she has worked in bronze, ceramics, and handmade paper, completing major sculpture commissions of cast bronze including the Edna Scott Foundation at Cowell College on the campus of the University of California at Santa Cruz. She studied at the University of California, Berkeley, and the California School of Fine Arts. When she was awarded the U.S./Japan Friendship Commission Grant, she was able to work, travel, and lecture in Japan. Her love of architecture and environmental design influences all her art (as can be seen in her work on the cover of this book), and has led to collaboration with her husband on the renovation of historic buildings. She and husband Tom live in Berkeley, where they raised their three children.

Rhoda Haas Goldman was born and grew up in San Francisco. She took her degree at U.C. Berkeley, where she lived in the just-completed Stern Hall, named for her grandmother. Her family has always been among U.C. Berkeley's most generous supporters. She married Richard N. Goldman and together they raised four children, hiked in Yosemite, and rafted many western rivers. And together she and Dick founded the extraordinary Goldman Environmental Prize. Often referred to as the Nobel Prize for the environment, these annual awards honor grass-roots environmental efforts on six continents. Few have contributed more to San Francisco life than Rhoda. She served as a director on many boards, was president of Mount Zion Hospital, the San Francisco Foundation, and Temple Emanu-El, chaired the finance committee of the San Francisco Symphony, and won awards in a variety of civic arenas. She still found time to be devoted to her family, and when she died in 1996 she left eleven grandchildren.

A native of San Francisco, **Kathryn Kendrick McNeil** raised five children of her own and became the stepmother to five more upon her second marriage. She loves everything out of doors and spends a lot of time hiking both in the North Carolina mountains, where she lives in the summer, and the Bay Area of San Francisco the rest of the year, with occasional trips to explore the landscapes of other continents. Her particular interest lies in the flora of wherever she happens to be, an enthusiasm that has led to her work as a distinguished docent at the Arboretum in Golden Gate Park. When not out of doors, she could well be pursuing her other ardent interest, writing, or keeping up with a growing number of grandchildren.

Rosemary Dundas Patton came to writing her own story after teaching writing in the English Department at San Francisco State University for fourteen years. Born in England, she moved to Scotland where, at eight, she vowed to become a writer. At twelve, with her three sisters, one brother, and her parents, she moved again, to North Carolina. She followed a B.A. in English from Duke University with an M.A. from San Francisco State several years later. By then she, her pediatrician husband Gray, and three daughters had settled in California. Today, the balance has shifted to include four young grandsons. Her vow to write was postponed many decades, but a college textbook, *Writing Logically, Thinking Critically*, launched her, and a recently discovered old letter from her English professor father-in-law validated her wishes: "Thank you for your wonderful letter; you are my favorite author."

Joann Maxwell Reinhardt was born in Indiana and moved to Southern California when she was six. Soon after graduating from Stanford, she moved to San Francisco, where she has continued to live except for year-long stays in Greece, Turkey, and Switzerland with her husband, author and journalist Richard Reinhardt. At various times she has been an elementary school teacher, a San Francisco guide, and the owner of a small cooking business. But her primary career has always been her home and family, grown from three sons to include three grandchildren. In addition to writing family memoirs, she loves to cook, and, with husband Dick, gardens at their weekend house in Sonoma County and enjoys world-wide travel.

Susan Wheelock Renfrew, born in Ohio, grew up in Michigan. She came to San Francisco in the 1950s with her lawyer-husband and has been well acquainted with boys as a second-grade teacher of thirty-eight children, an art teacher at a facility for emotionally disturbed boys, mother of three boys, and grandmother to two. Luckily, she also has a daughter and three granddaughters. Currently single, she leads seminars on art, music, and psychology in a Jungian Center north of San Francisco, is enjoying world travel, and when her son-in-law, ever helpful with the computer, doesn't send her stories "bye-bye" (his words) into cyberspace, she likes writing her memoirs.

Jean-Louise Naffziger Thacher (Beenie) was born and raised in San Francisco. She received a B.A. in Psychology from Stanford, worked for the American Red Cross and for a book publisher in New York. She continued her education by marrying a U.S. Foreign Service Officer, living first in Pakistan, and then in Philadelphia, India, Washington, D.C., Iraq, Iran, and Saudi Arabia with their three children. Memoir writing usually concentrates on those rich and varied years of her life and allows her to share the experiences with her family and friends. She keeps her ties to the Middle East alive by working on a bibliography of Arabic literature. And now she is learning about America in the 1990s from her six grandchildren (including twin boys) while living with her husband on San Francisco's Nob Hill.

Mary Wilbur Thacher says of herself: "I remember so little of my childhood because I had such a blissfully happy one." She lived first on Vallejo Street in San Francisco where children from the hills around would gather to play hide and seek and kick the can, and where she walked up a steep hill to the Grant Public School, all of San Francisco Bay spread out below. Then in fourth grade she moved to Burlingame on the San Francisco Peninsula. After six years at a Sacred Heart convent, she went east to Vassar College, a quite overwhelming experience for a girl from the West. She finished at the University of California, Berkeley, and finally managed to marry a man who "met my parents' approval." They live in San Francisco, where she devotes considerable time to the arts, but they spend as much time as possible in Sonoma. Two of their children live nearby in the Napa Valley, one in the Northwest. A few years ago she spent some time contemplating what "I would do if I were penniless." She finally decided that she would open "Mary's Truck Stop." She claims she can cook good breakfasts, soups, and pies. In other words, she'd make a good short-order cook. After all, that is what "I have been doing all my married life."

Olive Gamble Waugh (Babs) was born in Berkeley, grew up in Los Angeles, received a B.A. from Stanford, and attended the University of Pennsylvania Medical School. She married a physician, whom she met in medical school, and has lived most of her adult life in San Francisco, raising two daughters there. She worked for a time as a research technician studying cardiac arrhythmias, then started a medical career program for high school students and, later, an adult literacy program, both of which are still flourishing. After she was widowed, she married again and lives with her husband in Los Altos Hills, south of San Francisco.

Betty Bird Whitridge moved on from "only child" in Arlington, Washington, to the University of Washington and then marriage to "a tall, handsome easterner, Fred" who had come west after college. They moved around for a number of years till they reached "Mecca," corporate headquarters in San Francisco, where they settled down, raised four sons, traveled extensively, and took part in the cultural and civic life of the city. They spent summers on Orcas Island in the San Juan Islands of Washington, and after retirement, moved to their property there, returning to their San Francisco house for only four winter months each year. No matter where she is, Betty has a spectacular garden, needlepoints every surface, sings with choral societies, reads at dazzling speed, supports her community, and with Fred, enjoys expanding and restoring their property. Somehow, she finds time to write about her life and entertain nine grandchildren.